GUIDE TO INTERNAL COMMUNICATION METHODS

Guide to Internal Communication Methods

Edited by Eileen Scholes
on behalf of The ITEM Group

Gower

Published by
Gower Publishing Limited
Gower House
Croft Road
Aldershot
Hampshire GU11 3HR
England

Gower
Old Post Road
Brookfield
Vermont 05036
USA

British Library Cataloguing in Publication Data

Guide to internal communication methods
  1. Communication in management
  I. Scholes, Eileen
  658.4'5

ISBN 0 566 08217 9

Library of Congress Cataloging-in-Publication Data
Guide to internal communication methods / edited by Eileen Scholes, on behalf of ITEM.
    p.   cm.
  Includes index.
  ISBN 0–566–08217–9 (hardback)
  1. Communication in personnel management.   2. Communication in management.
  I. Scholes. Eileen.
  HF5549.5.C6G83   1999
  658.4'5—dc21

                                                            99–17211
                                                              CIP

Phototypeset in 10 point Palatino by Intype London Ltd and printed in Great Britain by MPG Ltd, Bodmin.

Contents

Editor's preface

This small book came out of a much larger one, the *Gower Handbook of Internal Communication* (1997).

That book has a role akin to that of an emerging country's first international airport. It's there to open up trading routes between a resource-rich but still relatively isolated community (that of professional communication) and a tougher, but potentially more rewarding world (that of strategic business management).

By contrast, the book you have in your hands is a private helicopter pad. Its job is to enable enterprising (or desperate) managers to fly direct to the heart of Internal Communication's mysterious interior – the 'how to' zone, where the quick wins lie.

Why this book is needed

The implementation side of communication – once a no-go area for the non-specialist – is fast becoming an area of core competence for all business managers and team leaders.

On the one hand, that's because technology (especially information technology) is coming together with improved knowledge of organizational/individual dynamics to open up a range of hitherto unimagined possibilities in mass communication and communication in group and one-to-one situations.

On the other hand, boards are increasingly adopting business strategies that rely on improved communication capability to meet a range of new competitive factors. These include:

- *rapid market shifts* leading to more mergers and partnerships and in turn to a need for faster embedding of change in process, culture and development

- *the emergence of the professional shareholder* and the need for more meaningful and transparent measurement of output through performance management systems of one kind or another
- *the search for a faster cycle of differentiation* through lower costs, faster output and consistent innovation patterns, resulting in flatter management structures, smaller workforces, empowerment and more outsourcing
- *the race to attract and retain key employee groups* feeding into pay/benefit restructuring, improved personal development and career pathing

Factors like these are changing the way communication is funded and managed at every level of organizations. The result is a much wider choice of opportunities to communicate – and a parallel increase in the challenge of making the right choices about when, who to and how.

Cutting lead times and costs, for example, calls for more than new tools and processes. It means making fundamental changes in how people communicate with each other – the frequency, the speed, the tone and style. And it's not just people inside the organization who are affected. The whole range of stakeholders needs to be taken into account.

How to make the book work for you

See the book as a reference tool rather than a read-through. Use it to help you consider how best to apply different media in different situations and, wherever possible, how to make the communication interactive, a common requirement of solutions today.

To help you reach your decisions and compare across media, each is reviewed in the following format:

- *Strengths*
  the medium's inherent advantages
- *Opportunities*
  innovative uses
  how it can be made more involving and interactive
- *Weaknesses*
  the medium's inherent weaknesses
- *Pitfalls*
  common mistakes when misusing this medium

- *Budget issues*
  some of the cost factors you will need to consider
- *Timescales*
  Some of the time factors you will need to consider
- *Activities*
  step-by-step checklist of tasks you will need to undertake
- *Feedback*
  how you can build feedback routes into the medium
- *Measurement*
  how you can measure the effectiveness of your communication
- *How to find out more*
  guidance on books, resources and associations you can use for further research before making your decision

A necessary health warning

Using the book will help you select, plan and manage your use of communication processes more successfully in pursuit of business aims. By presenting you with an array of hard-won experience about what works and doesn't in different situations, it will help you become an effective and financially sound decision-maker about communication processes.

What the book won't do is make you a magazine editor or a conference producer or a trainer. I would argue that such people are largely born not made. They also require a currency and depth of technical knowledge and experience that those who manage communication on behalf of businesses neither need nor can afford to be distracted by.

So don't be seduced (or seduce yourself) into thinking you should do it all alone. Recognize your talent as that of an orchestral conductor. Without you, even the most brilliant ensemble of musicians will descend into unmusical chaos. Remember, it's more often the Simon Rattles of this world, and only rarely the bassoonists, who get the credit when the curtain comes down.

Eileen Scholes

Acknowledgements

The original concept for reviewing different media according to their strengths and weaknesses was Mike Long's. Tony Newbold was a close collaborator on both the content and writing of Part III of the *Gower Handbook of Internal Communication* on which this text is largely based. Sheila Hirst, Hugh Price and Alex Bund subjected the text of particular sections to expert review. The idea of producing this book came from Malcolm Stern of Gower, who deserves a medal for his patience and persistence.

1 Face-to-face communication

Formal meetings
One-to-one meetings
Team briefing
Mentoring, shadowing, secondment and visits
Walking the talk
Managed meals

FORMAL MEETINGS

Despite the innovations of new technologies, the personal interaction that takes place in face-to-face meetings remains an essential part of all human activity. Yet meetings are also classic time-wasters, with people leaving them feeling that nothing has been achieved.

This is often because not enough preparation has gone into the event, for example agreeing the aims, and circulating the agenda and any written materials in advance. Meetings can and should result in clear actions, responsibilities and deadlines, so that not only can the project move on, but people can feel motivated to play their part.

Strengths
- rapidly developing a shared vision
- gauging progress towards a vision
- gathering and exchanging information
- practical demonstrations or exercises are possible
- receiving immediate feedback
- clarifying accountabilities and agreeing actions
- fast problem-solving, for example at project team meetings
- strengthening relationships

Opportunities
- set agendas
  - give all participants a chance to influence the objectives of the meeting
- manage participation
  - an effective chairperson will draw out all participants by inviting them to contribute, or by asking questions
- share presentation
  - divide the burden of presenting information and produce documentation to help add variety and involve more of the participants
- circulate reading materials in advance
  - everyone needs notice so that they can read, digest and assess relevant materials to be able to make a full contribution to the meeting
- use techniques such as brainstorming to tap creativity and involve everyone
- bring a fresh perspective by involving people from

outside the team, for example customers, suppliers or people from different departments
- break the meeting into subgroups to tackle particular issues and reconvene
- messages from the meeting can be angled and communicated on to target audiences, making them feel involved

Weaknesses
- can be time-consuming
- difficult to coordinate diaries – may result in delay
- traditionally poorly handled, resulting in low expectations from participants

Pitfalls
- late starts
  - typical of internal meetings, this adds greatly to the real cost
  - time discipline is vital, so do not be tempted to be too generous when waiting for latecomers
- poor location
  - for example poor lighting, noise, inadequate seating
- unclear aim
  - objective not agreed/agenda not circulated in advance
- irrelevant topics
  - have you invited the right people for this subject area?
- overloaded agenda
  - better to have shorter meetings more often than infrequent long meetings
- the meeting dives into detail
  - detail is better handled through written communication, circulated before or after the meeting
- wrong time balance
  - too much time is devoted to a low-priority issue
  - individual items may be too long, resulting in fatigue and boredom: you may be able to break them down into smaller, better-defined subjects
  - schedule in natural mind-breaks, even at short meetings, giving people a chance to recharge before the next topic
  - think carefully about allocating time in the agenda: you can be flexible on the day, but you can postpone a tricky item rather than sacrifice the rest of the business of the meeting
- poor chairing, carrying the risk of:
  - overrunning, or some items being rushed through

– sidetracking
– conflict
– poor participation with a few people dominant
– no agreed outcomes or actions

Budget issues
- time spent on meeting preparation, and producing and circulating documents
- participants' time at the meeting
  – are all these people needed?
  – would a smaller group achieve more, faster?
- any travel cost and time
  – could the meeting be handled by an e-mail conference, a round-robin memo, or phone and fax?
- opportunity cost incurred while participants are at the meeting
  – for example lost production or sales
- meeting room overheads, refreshments, materials
- time spent on minuting the meeting and producing summary documents

Timescales
- formal meetings need at least two weeks to set up to allow people to organize diaries, consider the agenda, and read any preparatory material
- for regular meetings plan two or three weeks ahead
- you can arrange urgent on-site meetings almost immediately

Activities
- define the meeting's objective
- determine if this objective can be better achieved in any other way
- propose meeting date and venue
- agree meeting date and venue
- circulate agenda, any documentation to read and any actions to be carried out before the meeting
- run the meeting, making sure that everybody is fully involved
- manage the time carefully, summarizing conclusions and agreeing action points before moving on to the next item
- summarize and close the meeting, highlighting any action points, deadlines and accountabilities
- circulate minutes of the meeting, including any actions to be taken as a result

Feedback
- immediate feedback at meeting
- include a questionnaire when circulating minutes

Measurement
- compare the meeting's outcome with its stated objectives
- research to identify best practice meetings and key benchmarks
  - share this information around the organization and, if appropriate, use 'star players' as coaches
- conduct regular cost-benefit analysis to judge effectiveness
  - so many of the real costs of a meeting are hidden that this is a useful discipline

How to find out more

How to Win Meetings by Greville Janner, Gower, 1990

Positive Management: assertiveness for managers by Paddy O'Brien, Nicholas Brealey Publishing/The Industrial Society, 1992

'Effective communication' by Paul Sandwith, *Training and Development* (USA), January 1992

Effective Meetings by P. Hodgson, Century, 1993

'Don't communicate – involve!' by Anne Evison, *Training and Development* (UK), June 1994

ONE-TO-ONE MEETINGS

As with all forms of face-to-face communication, one-to-one meetings carry maximum exposure for both participants, but also offer the highest potential for communicating and checking understanding.

In a management context they represent a significant investment of management time, and as such tend to be used for specific purposes such as recruitment and appraisal interviews, coaching, counselling and mentoring. The success of the meeting hinges chiefly on the ability, experience and training of the manager running the meeting, and the thought he or she has put into planning it.

Strengths
- personal and direct
- can deal with sensitive or 'off-the-record' subjects
- closely targeted on the needs and interests of both people
- should be highly interactive
  - questions, answers and feedback on both sides
- instant feedback and reaction
- you can check understanding and agreement on the spot, without interruption
- can be informal and relaxed to build relationships and motivation
- practical demonstrations or exercises possible

Opportunities
- be aware of how your body language can reinforce what you are saying
- talk through visuals or documents together
- be flexible enough to tailor the meeting more closely to the emerging needs of the other person
- listen actively and ask open questions
- summarize regularly to check understanding and agreement
- one-to-one meetings can be very frank and revealing
  - for example with careful planning exit interviews can give very valuable 'from the horse's mouth' information about how the organization is working

Weaknesses
- time-consuming
- can be threatening for both parties
  - their skills and personalities are on the line
- relies on ability and credibility of the manager/leader

- sometimes old hostilities and personality clashes can arise, which would be tempered by the presence of a neutral mediator or diplomat

Pitfalls
- assuming that because the other party is not saying much, they are in agreement
- not recording the meeting
  - both parties leave with an entirely different view of what has been agreed
- paying so much attention to running the meeting that you are not listening to what the other person is saying

Budget issues
- time spent on meeting preparation and circulating documents
- participants' time at the meeting
- travel cost and time
- opportunity cost incurred while participants are at the meeting
  - for example lost production or sales
- meeting room overheads, refreshments, materials
- time spent writing reports or filling in forms

Timescales
- can be instant, sitting by someone's workstation
- formal one-to-one meetings, like appraisal interviews, require weeks of notice, so that both parties can prepare

Activities
- set objectives
- for formal one-to-one meetings agree a time, and a quiet venue
- ensure that you will not be interrupted
- allocate time for different subjects
- if there is anything relevant for the other person to prepare or read, ask them to do this before they come
- run the meeting, making it as participative as possible, checking agreement and understanding as you go
- summarize the outcome of the meeting, agreements reached and actions to be taken
- where appropriate, follow up with a written summary of what was agreed

Feedback
- immediate feedback at the meeting
- follow-up questionnaire
  - giving anything but positive feedback at a one-to-one meeting could be interpreted as a challenge or personal criticism of the manager
  - it may be safer to direct honest and open feedback

into a formatted questionnaire with a rating system, giving *both* sides an opportunity to 'score' the meeting

Measurement

• compare the meeting's outcome with its stated objective

How to find out more

Effective Meetings by P. Hodgson, Century, 1993
How to Win Meetings by Greville Janner, Gower, 1990
Talking from 9 to 5: how women's and men's conversational styles affect who gets heard, who gets credit, and what gets done at work by Deborah Tannen, Virago, 1995
Tough Talking: how to handle awkward situations by David Martin, Pitman Publishing, 1993

TEAM BRIEFING

Team briefing has had its critics. However, it is a persistently popular way for organizations to cascade information out from the centre, through a network of managers, supervisors and team leaders, to reach all employees.

Used effectively it can offer the best of all worlds, being an ideal way to promote employees' understanding of key issues, and providing a platform to feed back information and views to the centre.

While many organizations use regular team briefing, the same principles can be applied to special one-off briefs, for example to address issues concerning a product launch, reorganization or relocation.

Strengths
- core business and organizational issues presented within a consistent framework but in a local context by a local leader
- face-to-face communication, employees' usual preferred method
- small, familiar group environment
- reinforces and builds on the natural work group structure
- can be highly interactive, with questions asked, ideas prompted or challenged and consensus arrived at on the spot
- understanding can be checked immediately
- corporate messages can be interpreted to make them directly relevant to the needs of the local audience
- team-specific issues can be raised and discussed
- enables teams to set goals and agree how to organize their work
- provides a forum for employees to raise concerns, ask questions and feed back their opinions and ideas

Opportunities
- has the potential to become the 'hub' of the organization's communication structure
- carefully formatted, can initiate new cultural styles and initiatives, for example greater interactivity, involvement
- properly adapted and personalized to the needs and interests of the workforce, can help to align personal

and business goals, inspire new commitment, energy and enthusiasm

- where appropriate, individuals can brief the others on their area of expertise
- carefully constructed briefing materials (see briefing packs, p. 53) support busy managers, enabling them to take ownership of messages
- provide photocopyable briefing sheets for passing out to employees as reinforcement or to provide detailed information
- involve the team in recording and minuting their own briefing
- build in a question and answer session
  - briefing packs should include answers to likely questions
  - encourage managers to be honest if they do not know the answer, and provide a rapid support service so they can promise to find out
- consider circulating briefing packs simultaneously at different levels, minimizing the inevitable delay with many-layered cascades
- chance for IC to get early access to senior management thinking on core issues

Weaknesses
- success is largely dependent on a complex range of wider organizational and cultural issues, like management structure, communication structure and equipment, relationships between the centre and operations, and whether interpersonal skills and 'bottom up' contributions have historically been valued and rewarded
- time-consuming and therefore costly
- relies on being able to pull a team together in the same place at the same time
- not suitable for conveying complex data
- relies on individual managers and leaders to be motivated and have the presentation and leadership skills to brief effectively in a 'formal' setting
- managers may distance themselves from unpleasant or difficult news, even to the extent of attacking and undermining senior management decisions

Pitfalls
- inconsistent messages given out (misdirects energy, loses credibility)
  - poor access to/support for senior management
  - low calibre/inexperienced creator of core brief

- managers do not know how to use the core briefing pack materials correctly
- lack of access to training
- can expose shortcomings of inexperienced or weak leaders or managers, or those used simply to giving instructions, affecting their credibility in other contexts
- opting for 'professional' or more senior level delivery loses the 'local' feel
- slow cascades
  - even with today's flatter hierarchies, it can still take a long time for the brief to trickle down from top management to line employee
  - if there is not as short a time as possible between the first and last person to be briefed, the grapevine will take over
- information dams
  - the cascade effectively breaks down if managers unilaterally decide to withhold information
  - careful monitoring is needed to identify sticking points and find out how to free up the information flow in future
- irregular briefing
  - briefings must be regular and deadlines kept to or the system will suffer and credibility will be lost
- boring delivery and irrelevant detail
  - poorly designed core brief
  - caused by managers not preparing adequately, not editing or personalizing the briefing pack material for their own team, or just reading it aloud verbatim with no expression or sense of ownership
  - monitor and measure to ensure all managers are performing to a consistently high standard, consider training for those who are not
- large groups
  - if team is larger than a dozen, ideally break it down into subgroups
  - ideal group size for participation is around six

Budget issues
- calibre of core briefing creator (good people cost more)
- time spent preparing and circulating briefs
- time spent on meeting preparation and circulating documents
- participants' time at the meeting
- travel cost and time
- opportunity cost incurred while participants are at the meeting

– for example lost production or sales
- meeting room overheads, refreshments, materials

Timescales
- team briefing can be very flexible depending on the needs of your organization
- regularity helps establish it as a valued communication method, for example on a rolling weekly, fortnightly or monthly programme
- some organizations may find it difficult to brief in under two weeks because of the time needed to generate and approve briefing packs
- urgent briefs can be prepared, distributed and delivered almost immediately, if the system is prepared for this (most likely using some form of electronic means)

Activities
- define objectives and outline content
- create core briefing pack (see briefing packs, p. 53), and submit for approval
- revise core briefing pack
- distribute core briefing pack
- local manager/leader combines core brief with local information and issues
- local manager personalizes core messages, making them more relevant to the local team
- manager hands out briefing pack summary for team
- manager conducts briefing, including question and answer and feedback sessions
- team minutes the briefing and any action points
- manager checks up on any unanswered questions and feeds back
- link into HR systems – induction, recruitment and promotion criteria, training provision/appraisals/ training needs analysis – to promote improved capability within the team at the sessions
- senior managers promote and validate the system whenever possible

Feedback
- immediate feedback at the briefing
- team leaders should also feed back their own opinions and pass on any relevant feedback from the team to the source of the brief

Measurement
- survey to measure retention of key messages
- employees rate team leader on his or her communication skill
- use focus groups to discuss attitudes to the briefing process and its effectiveness

- study under regular communication audit
- vital to measure and compare performance of different managers, and establish best practice managers as role models

How to find out more

Team Briefing, The Industrial Society, 1995

A Briefer's Guide to Team Briefing, The Industrial Society, 1990

Talking to the team (video), The Industrial Society/Video Arts, 1989

The Effective Communicator by John Adair, The Industrial Society, 1988

'The benefits of talking shop' by Lucie Carrington, *Personnel Today*, 17–30 May 1994

Employee Communications by Patrick Burns, The Industrial Society, 1994

The Industrial Society, Robert Hyde House, 48 Bryanston Square, London W1H 7LN 0171-262 2401

MENTORING, SHADOWING, SECONDMENT AND VISITS

The key to communication is understanding other people's needs, and putting yourself in their shoes, so that sender and receiver are literally 'on the same wavelength'. Mentoring, shadowing, secondment and visits all help people develop better insight into others' expectations, and help build and strengthen relationships.

Enabling greater personal contact between people of different grades and functions helps to enhance communication skills as well as promote communication across, up and down the organization. It helps challenge preconceptions, and give a real picture of the work of different functions.

Strengths
- personal and direct
- gives people a 'hands-on' feel, a direct sharing of experiences
- fully interactive

Opportunities
- visits from customers to meet employees, give talks, work in project teams, and give their feedback on performance
- customer placements
  - representative employees visit customers to gain insight into their operational needs
- mentoring provides an opportunity for direct two-way communication between protégé and coach
- shadowing
  - key employees shadow or swap with managers in different jobs, or different operations
  - this experience should be followed by written or face-to-face reports, including to the employee's own team
- site and function swaps
  - key staff swap between operations for short periods to give an insight into how other areas work
  - promotes understanding of other functions and departments
- local visits from senior management, ideally getting a

sense of life in the field, watching and talking to
employees about their views and concerns (see walking
the talk, p. 18)
  – while it is important to take a fairly structured
    approach, the schedule needs to be flexible enough
    to allow informal contact
• work placement
  – senior directors from companies like McDonalds and
    DHL are seconded for a day a year to work out in the
    field – it gives them real insight into the issues faced
    in the front line, and sends a strong team message
    to employees

Weaknesses
• time-consuming
• disrupts the host's normal schedule

Pitfalls
• no automatic follow-up
  – it is important for people to feel that their views have
    been listened to, and taken into account
• *'what on earth are* you *doing here?'*
  – if the objectives of the contact are unclear from all
    sides, it reduces the task to a 'social' visit

Budget issues
• time spent on preparation and contact
• lost working time

Timescales
• simple, short-term projects like in-house work
  placements can be set up within a week
• in general, time is needed to ensure that everyone is
  prepared, the objectives thought through and, where
  appropriate, the event is fully planned

Activities
• clarify objectives
• negotiate with target host or coach
• agree procedures and deadlines
• initiate the project and monitor
• plan and initiate any follow-up actions

Feedback
• direct feedback through personal contact

Measurement
• regular evaluation of the exercise by all participants
  – for example by questionnaires or surveys

**How to find out
more**
Everyone Needs a Mentor by David Clutterbuck, IPD, 1985
Mentoring in Action by David Clutterbuck and David
    Megginson, Kogan Page, 1995
Mentoring by Reg Hamilton, The Industrial Society, 1993
Mentoring: a guide to the basics by G. Shea, Kogan Page,
    1992

The European Mentoring Centre, Burnham House, High Street, Burnham, Bucks SL1 7JR 01628 661667 or Fax 01628 604 882

WALKING THE TALK

'Walking the talk' is a popular and vital part of people management. Typically, it involves managers scheduling time to walk around the workplace, talking to their team members, coaching and checking performance, motivating and listening to concerns, and gauging opinions.

Done well, it should help build an atmosphere of trust and strengthen relationships, giving the impression of a manager who is both on the ball and on the team.

Strengths
- enables immediate upwards feedback
- handled well, it is a good opportunity to boost credibility
- acts as a safety valve, enabling people to let off steam
- demonstrates concern for others' views
- provides high visibility through direct and personal contact
- shows that you are in touch with the workplace

Opportunities
- apply the principle in reverse by keeping an open door policy
- prepare a clear agenda for the conversation, but give people room to raise issues of their own
- extend the idea up and down the chain, visiting key suppliers and customers

Weaknesses
- relies heavily on the interpersonal skills of the manager
- assumes manager has easy access to the people on the team
- usually treated as a fairly unstructured exercise, hard to measure, with anecdotal benefits
- employees may feel rejected if not talked to
- some people may feel intimidated
- exposes managers with poor attitudes or weak interpersonal skills

Pitfalls
- *'of course I know my team are happy: they'd tell me otherwise'*
  - leaders sometimes assume their team members can be completely open with them, and are not intimidated by their status
- *'I just go in there and press the flesh'*
  - walking the talk depends upon having a clear

objective for talking with people, taking note of
their views and feeding those views upwards
- *'oh no, what have I done wrong now?'*
  - people need positive reinforcement
  - if the main reason a manager talks in depth to an
    employee is to correct them, you need not be
    surprised if they are guarded or defensive when
    talking to them
- *'we're expecting royalty'*
  - local leaders sometimes brief their teams to be on
    best behaviour and tell them what subjects to
    avoid, ensuring the visitor an upbeat but unrealistic
    experience
- *'time to get out the dirty washing'*
  - cynical employees may take the opportunity to stir
    up trouble, or undermine the visit
- *'going through the motions . . .'*
  - managers pay lip-service to the process,
    demotivating people by not really listening to them
  - points raised but unanswerable at the time of the
    encounter are not followed through and are simply
    forgotten about (by the manager)

Budget issues
- management and employee time

Timescales
- immediate, though a complete sweep of employees will
  need to take place on a rolling schedule

Activities
- facilitate the process of setting objectives/expectations,
  where possible both with the manager and with the
  team
- help managers think through the approach they need
  to take to get the results they want from individual
  team members
- encourage managers to watch, talk and listen to
  selected employees on a regular basis
- help managers rehearse with peers, or by themselves
  with a tape-recorder to see how they sound
- encourage managers to recognize where their weaker
  interpersonal skill areas lie and build them into
  personal development planning
- check back to see whether promises to seek out further
  information have been followed through

Feedback
- immediate and two-way, in conversation with the team
  member
- keeping employees informed of any new information
  of actions resulting from the conversation

Measurement
- attitude or opinion surveys before and after walkabouts
  - some teams are beginning to set up regular monitoring of managers' or leaders' behaviour to the rest of the team over an agreed period: feedback is usually via a scoresheet based on agreed criteria
- some managers use a log to assess how useful any data gathered is, and its impact on the organization's performance

How to find out more

The One Minute Manager by Ken Blanchard and S. Johnson, Fontana, 1983

Interpersonal Skills by Astrid French, The Industrial Society, 1993

The Industrial Society, Robert Hyde House, 48 Bryanston Square, London W1H 7LN 0171–262 2401

MANAGED MEALS

The Chinese have a saying: *we communicate by eating together*. Small groups are invited to discuss work issues with senior managers over special 'meals' on a rotating basis. Ideally they set people in the right frame of mind for creative, unhindered exchange of views, and provide a relaxed atmosphere and environment. Like all social occasions, there is a real opportunity for bridge-building, and getting to the heart of the matter, though if badly handled it can seem ritualistic, formal and unnatural.

Strengths
- high perceived value as an opportunity for frank two-way communication
- plays to some managers' strengths in one-to-one or one-to-group communication
- chance for employees to hear the 'big picture' as management views it
- demonstrates management concern to hear employee views
- can allow relaxed discussion of sensitive issues and sharing of experiences
- can be used to reward and recognize people's performance

Opportunities
- off-site venues
  - for example at a hotel, or at a customer's or supplier's premises, or even combined with a day-trip or picnic
- special events held during meal breaks
  - can be used for series of sessions, for example using outside speakers or a 'surgery' on benefits topics

Weaknesses
- the logistics can be complicated
  - you need the right mix of people, in the right place, at the right time, with the right menu
- people may feel pressured into attending, but forcing them would be counterproductive
- likely that because of the timing it will take place in someone's own time
- danger that poor food or service may undermine the exercise
- danger that free food may be the main motivator for attendance
- can have an unnatural 'captain's table' feel to it

- some people may find the idea offensive – 'I choose who I eat with'

Pitfalls
- *'why wasn't I invited?'*
  - if the events are being run on the basis of inviting a sub-section of the internal audience management is interested in, you need to make it clear to those not attending that the intention is to invite a *representative* sample: not being chosen has no reflection on their status, contribution or potential
- *'we've nothing in common'*
  - some managers are poor at 'small talk' or at communicating in small groups: they are better 'on stage'
  - exposing differences of views, or of language or style, can cause lasting gulfs between people
  - some employees will find the experience intimidating or even humiliating

Budget issues
- people's time
  - breakfast or evening events could be scheduled partly in working time, partly in people's own time
- cost of venue, food, service

Timescales
- *ad hoc* lunches can be arranged almost instantly, but more organized lunches may take at least a month to set up

Activities
- help managers set the objective for the meal and make this clear to people in the invitation
- explore the logistics
  - time, place, number of people, length of meal, catering arrangements
- determine who should be invited, and how (ensure people's line managers are informed and supportive)

Feedback
- direct feedback during the meal
- keep the attendees informed of any action resulting from their feedback

Measurement
- measure change in attitudes

How to find out more
The Industrial Society, Robert Hyde House, 48 Bryanston Square, London W1H 7LN 0171-262 2401

2 Events

Conferences
Presentations and speeches
Roadshows, themed events and business
simulations
Workshops and seminars

CONFERENCES

Much of the real 'business' of conferences tends to happen in the bars, restaurants and hotel lobbies. These are the places where relationships between colleagues are forged, renewed and strengthened. But a good conference can achieve more than teambuilding. With thorough planning and clear objectives, it can be a powerful force for motivating and channelling the talent of the entire organization.

Strengths
- off the job, away from day-to-day pressure
- effectively face to face, most people's preferred medium
- same set of messages to many at once – avoids Chinese whispers
- opportunity to 'hear it from the horse's mouth'
- opportunity for leadership
- builds group identity
- promotes shared organizational vision and values
- opportunity to ask questions – and to get immediate feedback
- chance to build trust and win commitment because everyone feels part of the process
- opportunity for peers from different areas or departments to come together
- promotes social and professional networking
- chance to reward, recognize and motivate people

Opportunities
- pre-conference preparation
  - research what target audiences want or need to know
  - ask delegates to read relevant documentation and choose which optional seminars and syndicates they want to attend
  - set them practical tasks in preparation for syndicates/workshops or seminars
- syndicates and workshops
  - break out into smaller groups to give more scope for participation and create a sense of involvement and ownership
- games and simulations will add variety and deal with management issues in more creative and interesting ways
- outside speakers
  - lend credibility or boost motivation by bringing in a

'best practice' expert or a high-powered speaker from outside
- open fora
  - senior managers circulate between small syndicate groups, giving people a chance to ask questions about all aspects of the organization
  - ideally should address a combination of pre-conference suggestions and questions arising from the conference itself
- post-conference action plans
  - delegates sign up to action plans, demonstrating their commitment to what was agreed at the conference, and transferring any learning back to the workplace
- social functions
  - ultimately these can make or break the atmosphere at a conference, and for many delegates are often the highlight
  - the social binding, grazing and teambuilding at parties has a positive impact, but ideally should be the final event of the conference, as the 'morning after' needs to be fairly undemanding
- conference voting systems
  - electronic voting systems are becoming more common, enabling 'straw polls' and votes on key issues from the audience, giving instant feedback
- creative effects
  - carefully crafted scenarios – maybe involving actors – and special effects can have a greater influence on audiences than straight 'speeches'
- post-conference cascade
  - promoting the vision and learning of the conference to the wider organization (see audiotape, p. 68, video, p. 76, multimedia, p. 98, briefing packs, p. 53)

Weaknesses
- require a great deal of preparation – one of the most demanding and politically exposed project management tasks for a communication provider
- high cost of lost work and opportunities
- reveals weak speakers
- gaffes are very public
- external venues too public or insecure for sensitive subjects

Pitfalls
- disappointing expectations
  - the very public loss of face in 'cancelling' or

'shrinking' a conference either in length or in numbers of delegates

- deciding the logistics before the objectives and content
  - you may be scraping the barrel to fill up a two-day programme, when one day would do
- poor technology management
  - there's nothing less impressive than microphones that don't work or give off high pitched screams, or special effects that don't come off
  - it's easy to underestimate the back-up needed for the highly sophisticated range of speaker support now available
- poor venue choice
  - service is as important as facilities; even today Basil Fawltys seem to be everywhere
  - after drawing up a short list, visit the venues (including unannounced visits to see how they *really* operate); meet the staff who will be looking after your delegates
  - put yourself in the delegates' shoes
  - imagine the logistics of the venue when dealing with your number of delegates (noise level, movement between rooms, telephone availability, serving times in the restaurant and so on)
- poor financial management
  - agree venue costs in *fine* detail
  - watch out for 'hidden extras' or variable costs at the venue like on-site photocopying charges, equipment hire
- *'but I thought you were talking on . . .'*
  - presenters often automatically agree to speak to the brief given them, and then on the day talk about something entirely different, because they don't focus on the task until the last minute
- poor attendance
  - all conferences have 'graveyard' slots, notably early morning, post-lunch and in the final sessions
  - the problem is exacerbated by the fact that poorer speakers tend to be given the poorly attended slots
  - it's possible to buck the trend by closing the conference with a keynote speech
- information overload
  - many presenters are tempted to shoehorn as much information into their presentations as possible, overloading the audience

- persuade them to move the detail into supporting documents (see presentations and speeches, p. 31)
- poor pacing
  - an ideal conference includes a mix of subjects and presentation styles – this is a strength that should be built on
  - aim to mix contrasting views, stimulating debate
  - place strategic breaks where the programme needs them, not when the venue 'deigns' to grant them
- lack of logic
  - where possible group presentations into themed sessions
- dire presentations
  - while presentation training can help, some people simply cannot present and undermine their own credibility and embarrass themselves, the audience and the organization as a whole
  - different presentation styles may help weaker presenters, for example by having them interviewed, on video, or working in partnership with a stronger co-presenter
  - a senior manager needs to take ownership of the programme, weeding out, vetting and project managing the presentations to ensure that standards are consistently high
- poor involvement
  - many conferences fall down in that far from *conferring*, people use it as an opportunity to talk *at* their colleagues
  - although most programmes rely heavily on speeches, good speakers involve the audience as they go, asking for examples, reactions and questions
  - programmes need an element of choice; aim to expose delegates to situations where they must take active part, such as workshops, seminars and syndicate groups

Budget issues
- decide who *really* needs to attend
  - can information be conveyed more effectively to non-attendees by video or briefing documents?
- anticipate *all* venue charges
- determine the balance of internal and external resourcing
- choose the right conference production company
- equipment hire
- travel and accommodation

- project management and administration time
- delegates' attendance time, travel time and any opportunity cost
- producing branded notepads, programmes, promotional material
- technical facilities
- set design and construction
- time and materials on preparing speeches, presentations, videos, workshops and syndicates
- contingency budget
  - because you are dealing with a fixed deadline, you need to budget for last minute emergencies, such as 'rush fees' for slide production, or hiring a special piece of equipment
- cost of external speakers, presenters and facilitators
- time and materials on supporting documentation
- time and materials on follow-up, feedback, measurement and analysis

Timescales
- a practical minimum of at least two months, but large conferences should be planned at least a year in advance
- the best venues and speakers are booked well in advance

Activities
- set and agree objectives of conference
- decide who needs to attend
- plan out proposed content, length and logistics
- win agreement for budget
- select a venue that fits the audience and activity requirements
- approach potential speakers and agree content outlines with them
- distribute and manage invitations
- organize any accommodation and supplementary activities
- organize any support materials needed
- set up at venue
- if possible, run through and time presentations
- organize set and speakers

Feedback
- questionnaires after individual sessions
- full questionnaire at end of conference
- follow-up questionnaire back at the workplace, away from the 'high' of the conference

Measurement
- track the speed and quality of information passed out to non-attendees, if appropriate

- measure attitude change before and after conference

How to find out more

How to Organize a Conference by Iain Maitland, Gower, 1996

How to Organise Effective Conferences and Meetings by David Seekings, Kogan Page, 1992

The Complete Conference Organiser's Handbook by Robin O'Connor, Piatkus, 1994

'Positive interaction' by Bridget Kelly, *Managing Service Quality*, November 1992

Association of Conference Executives, Riverside House, High St, Huntingdon, Cambs PE18 6SG 01480 457595

PRESENTATIONS AND SPEECHES

Presentations and speeches are the principal media at most events. While the information content they can carry is fairly limited, they can have a powerful impact on an emotional level, especially when supported by striking graphics, lighting, sound, choreographed events and stagecraft.

Strengths
- personal and direct
- good for creating an emotional commitment, motivating audiences

Opportunities
- autocue, with speech text projected onto a screen or lectern
  - enables the speaker to make regular eye contact with the audience, making them feel more involved
- use a link-person to be the audience's representative on stage, summarizing key points and asking for clarification when needed
- roving mike
  - allows experienced presenters to circulate among the audience, asking for questions, comments or examples
  - imposes a useful discipline – only the person with the microphone is supposed to be speaking
  - gives audience members a feeling of equal status with the speaker
  - etiquette is important, organizers should try to ensure that no one 'hogs' the microphone and that a variety of people manage to talk
- written documents
  - these will be the lasting memory of the presentation
  - use these to carry any facts and figures you want to convey but were too complex for the speech, and include paper copies of overheads or slides
- video and audiotape
  - these can capture the flavour and style of the presentation, recording them for a wider audience

Weaknesses
- poor at conveying complex ideas, facts and figures
  - use written documentation to support the key messages of the presentation
- high risk, high exposure

    – a poor performance will embarrass the speaker, the organization and the audience
- limited to conveying only a few key messages
- in most cases, limited scope for widespread participation, although taking every opportunity for interaction will help, for example asking questions

Pitfalls
- *'what I want to talk to you about today is . . .'*
  - many speakers fail to put themselves in the audience's shoes
  - they don't even ask who the audience is
  - they don't research to find out what they want to hear
  - if they've been given a brief they may well ignore it
- lack of a clear brief from the organizer, including the audience's profile, and any information about their needs
- eleventh hour presentation style
  - many presenters underestimate how long it will take them to produce their presentations, and can result in extra costs for 'rush' fees for overheads
  - organizers need to check regularly on progress, for example asking to see a synopsis at an early stage to ensure that it matches the brief
- mix and match
  - presenters try to recycle a mix of old presentations, and cannibalize any material they can find
  - this runs the risk of not meeting the audience's needs, and it becomes obvious when there are sudden changes in style, tone and subject matter
- overrunning
  - a common problem, resulting from lack of preparation and focus
  - it looks unprofessional, inconveniences the audience and any co-presenters and carries the risk of skipping over key messages
- diving into detail
  - experts disappear down detailed sidetracks that the audience may not be able to follow
  - the problem can usually be tracked back to the synopsis, which attempts to cover too many points in too much detail
- prose
  - speakers often create their presentations as prose on paper, whereas the aim is for spoken English
  - many speeches sound like turgid academic or

business reports, with very little active language, great formality and endless subclauses that make the spoken sentence almost impossible to follow
- style over substance
  - presenters fall in love with a glitzy theme, and bend their messages to fit
  - too much glitz can get in the way of clarity
- stage fright
  - this is surprisingly common among managers
  - nervous presentation style and body language transmits to the audience, making them nervous too
  - advise speakers to avoid alcohol or tranquillizers
  - there is no 'cure' as such, other than a combination of painful experience, rehearsal and specialized presenter training courses
- runaway train
  - nerves and lack of preparation can cause presenters to deliver their material at a relentless pace, incomprehensible to the audience
  - timing is vital, and the only accurate way to time a presentation is to rehearse thoroughly

Budget issues
- time and materials on producing the speech, and supporting documents and visuals
- venue costs
- time spent at the venue
- travel time and cost
- time spent on follow-up, for example sending further information on request to delegates

Timescales
- many presenters do produce speeches literally the night before, which is precisely why the general standard is so low
- to stand out from the crowd, a speaker needs to start compiling a presentation at least a month in advance
  - the more time the speaker gives themselves, the more opportunity they have to put the script down, and come at it afresh, improving the quality of their revisions

Activities
- set objectives
- confirm time and venue for the presentation
- get the speaker to produce any written support they may want to give their audience – leave-behinds and handouts
- outline the content of the presentation

- revise outline
- draft presentation
- revise draft
  - read draft aloud for timing and to reveal areas where it does not flow
- draft out visual support
- produce visual support, for example overheads, slides or any props
  - depending on how you are producing visuals, the content needs to be finalized fairly early in the process as they can take one or two weeks to produce
- revise draft and if necessary reduce to bullet points or write speaker's notes on cards
- rehearse and revise
  - keep doing this until you are satisfied that the speech has impact and that it's at the target length

Feedback
- tape record or video-record a rehearsal
  - *the speaker* will be their own most powerful critic
- test presentations on colleagues or family
- gauge immediate audience reaction on the day
- if appropriate, give the audience sheets to fill in on speaker performance

Measurement
- retention of key messages
- speaker performance by questionnaire

How to find out more
Effective Presentation by Antony Jay, Pitman, 1993
Janner's Complete Speechmaker by Greville Janner, Century, 1991

ROADSHOWS, THEMED EVENTS AND BUSINESS SIMULATIONS

Roadshows, themed events and business simulations are increasingly popular ways of reaching internal audiences with high profile materials and imaginative practical sessions.

Strengths
- a roadshow delivers consistent messages, touring to reach people at different sites with the same materials
- themed events can 'spice up' ordinary messages
- business simulations give people a chance to 'discover' messages for themselves as the simulation unravels

Opportunities
- annual event
  - opportunity for senior management to meet people, rather like an AGM for shareholders, concentrating on the organization's performance
- question and answer fora
  - opportunity to raise issues and concerns with the 'people who know'
  - frequently asked questions can be summarized, and used as the basis for further research, or the answers established
- roadshow presentations
  - for example senior managers out on the road to different locations
  - especially important in organizations where senior management is centralized, far from many employees/ suppliers/franchisees etc.

Weaknesses
- relatively high cost
- a roadshow can take a long time to reach a number of sites
- different themes tend to appeal to different people
- managers are taken away from their jobs for long periods

Pitfalls
- simulations too generic or too specific
  - business simulations work best when they relate directly to the needs and experience of the audience
  - opting for a generic exercise carries the danger that the simulation won't *directly* relate to any one audience, but it should at least be recognizable to all

                   – opting for a specific exercise carries the danger that the simulation may relate well to one group, but not another
                   – where possible, simulations should be a mix of generic skills and issues, customized for specific audiences

Budget issues

Roadshow
- designing and producing the roadshow and exhibition
- organizing, producing and presenting roadshow events
- travel costs, time and accommodation
- creating any support materials, for example brochures

Themed events
- creating and testing the theme
- project managing and producing the event
- creating any support materials

Business simulations
- creating, testing, revising and using the simulation
- producing any support materials, for example handouts and workbooks

Timescales
- allow at least three months to plan roadshows, themed events and business simulations, depending on the scale of the project

Activities
- set objectives
- design event, roadshow materials or simulation
- implement and assess

Feedback
- feedback gathered through discussion at roadshows, and participation through themed events and simulations

Measurement
- retention of key messages
- profile of audience reached by roadshow

How to find out more

How to Organise Effective Conferences and Meetings by David Seekings, Kogan Page, 1992

Association of Conference Executives, Riverside House, 160 High St, Huntingdon, Cambs PE18 6SG 01480 457595

WORKSHOPS AND SEMINARS

Workshops and seminars are used as a semi-formal way to involve people more actively at events. The two terms are moving closer together, as seminars are becoming more participative and less academic.

Strengths
- small groups
- personal contact
- highly interactive
- practical and focused
- flexible
  - you can use workshops to focus on specific, local team issues, or to give local people perspective on the wider organization

Opportunities
- involving the wider team
  - if appropriate to the objective, invite customers or suppliers to give their input too
- customizing the workshop
  - ask people to prepare before the workshop, bringing along a project or task of their own that reflects their individual needs
- sharing the seminar workload
  - moving away from the academic image of a seminar, as effectively speech-giving to a small group, to a full participation event, with tasks allocated between all participants
- winning levels of buy-in from broad agreement through to acceptance of proposed solutions and actions

Weaknesses
- time-consuming
- likely inconsistency between events as the outcomes and success depend on the work and attitudes of the individual groups

Pitfalls
- the wrong people
  - workshops and seminars need to attract the people who will be able to make a difference, and motivate them to do so, otherwise you risk 'preaching' to the 'converted' or the 'disenfranchised'
  - an inappropriate topic would alienate the audience

Budget issues
- opportunity cost of people's time
- time and materials in preparing, designing and running
  - many materials will be generated by the teams at the workshop, and these will need to be edited after the event
- time of all participants
- cost of venue and refreshments

Timescales
- allow at least a few days to book time in people's diaries, and to design and set up a workshop
- allow one month for a seminar

Activities

Workshop
- set objectives
- produce and distribute the agenda or outline
- select participants
- select and organize venue
- identify exercises and demonstrations
- design workshop and schedule
- produce any supporting materials
- run the workshop
- record actions and issues arising
- edit and circulate materials produced by the teams
- follow up any agreed actions

Seminar
- set objective
- produce and distribute the agenda or outline
- select participants
- ideally, all participants should have a clear role, for example a presentation to make
- chair to ensure full participation
- produce any supporting documents or visuals

Feedback
- immediate feedback at the event
- questionnaire when back in the workplace to gauge the application of key messages in daily work
- distribution of agreed actions, and follow-up meetings to see how they were carried out

Measurement
- retention of key messages
- performance improvements in target areas

How to find out more
How to run Seminars and Workshops by R. L. Jolles, John Wiley & Sons, 1994
Workshops that Work by Tom Bourner, McGraw-Hill, 1993

3 Print-based communication

Magazines and newspapers
Newsletters
Manuals, guides and handbooks
Brochures and reports
Briefing packs

MAGAZINES AND NEWSPAPERS

With IC's range widening to include more face-to-face communication, regular publications (periodicals) generally have taken something of a back seat.

For most organizations, however, their regular newspaper or magazine still acts as the symbol of their existence as a community. It is one of the few forums where everyone – managers as well as others – come together on a virtually equal footing as members of 'a club'. As such, it can become a clear 'voice' for the organization, embodying its values and beliefs.

Thanks to the flexibility of publications, content can be funny, sad and serious all at the same time. It can cover a range of subject matter, from important management statements to pictures of a social event.

Modern-style publications place emphasis on the exchange of best practice and a greater element of interaction all round. And, though the vast majority are print-based, many are moving towards video, multimedia or intranet formats.

Format distinctions between newspapers and magazines have become blurred in recent years. In the past, the choice between a newspaper/magazine format for employees was simply based on 'what we assume our people read outside'. For manufacturing and retail staff, for example, managers' knee-jerk assumption was (and to an extent still is) 'tabloid'.

Several developments have opened up opportunities to approach this issue in more sophisticated ways, starting from what the business wants to achieve. One big factor behind the new flexibility is the fact that changes have been occurring on the news-stands.

Despite the tabloids' self-created high profile, publishers know that the real growth in the British reading market over the past 10 years, across all social groupings, has actually been in magazines. The women's magazine sector has grown – while also becoming more fragmented – but the most startling growth has been in men's and special interest magazines. Evidence of this increasing interest is that most newspapers, including many tabloids, now include magazines as part of their offer.

The conclusion has to be that most people (men and women) who regularly buy and read publications, regularly access both newspapers and magazines with equal ease and familiarity.

So – when to use which? If you want to maintain interest, manage expectations and maintain credibility with a particular audience, the important thing to decide is *why* and *in what circumstances* people would choose to read the publication – and therefore in which format.

Take a look at some of the principal differences in expectation inherent in the two formats.

Newspapers
- rely on high impact material (headlines and photography)
- style, language and assumed education level is closely targeted to particular socio-economic groups
- high frequency (low frequency of internal newspapers often seen as a joke by employees)
- here today gone tomorrow treatment of subjects
- don't bother to keep or take home
- tend to 'come down on one side' on issues
- must have lots of small snippets (requires large contact networks; heavy on time/cost to collect)
- 'behind the news' treatments less about 'understanding' than adding narrative detail and extra human interest
- real newspapers are printed on cheap, relatively flimsy paper stock (called newsprint): organizations tend to confuse readers' expectations by upgrading the paper quality

Magazines
- less about 'new' information, more about people and issues 'in the news'
- readers share an interest but can come from all education levels, backgrounds, e.g. *Motorcycle News*
- seen as a mix of seeking increased understanding, 'behind the scenes' information/education, entertainment
- 'keep it and read again' feel
- more flexibility – more scope for feature treatments as well as shorter items
- less 'news' expectation, only topicality

- bi-monthly frequency seen as 'normal' on a magazine
- easier to go up or down in size – works equally well at either 12 or 16 pages
- colour taken as standard
- usually higher quality stock than 'newsprint'

Strengths
- familiar format and style
- can be read anywhere at any time
- reaches all audiences
- easy to distribute personal copies
- flexible in terms of content and style

Opportunities
- letters pages, anonymous if appropriate
- questions and answers with senior managers, revealing areas of complaint
- clear, regular format – people can find the information they need as quickly as possible
- targeted publications
  - 'opt-out' pages enabling customized content, for example special pages for individual sites
  - entire publications aimed at a particular group of employees, customers or suppliers
- reader services
  - discounts, for example trips, products and services, small ads, free samples
- special issues and inserts
  - newspaper and magazines become special 'brands' which recipients recognize instantly
  - their strength can be built on by issuing supporting documents under the same brand, or special 'stop press' newsletters to address urgent issues
- print on demand
  - improvements in print technology, and its flexibility, mean that it is becoming increasingly feasible to create printed media with shorter print runs, aimed at the needs of niche groups
  - a master copy of the magazine or newspaper is stored on disk or digitally scanned at a centre and transmitted to sites right across the world, the sites then print it – this cuts out any distribution delay, meaning that everyone gets the news fast, and at the same time.

Weaknesses
- relatively slow
- although they may mimic the format of news-stand newspapers and magazines, the content is almost

bound to be of less general interest, and the design and journalistic standards can be inferior

Pitfalls
- newspapers can give a 'downmarket' impression, and use 'downmarket' content
- they can be perceived as propaganda, even when not
- legal, honest, decent and true?
  - management can indeed fall into the trap of behaving like media barons, spreading their own propaganda
- traditional newspapers/magazines actually have very little direct reader involvement; classically trained journalist/editors may find it hard to change their approach

Budget issues
- for large organizations, it may be possible to subsidize the magazine or newspaper with advertisements
- project-managing an internal newspaper or magazine is complex and time-consuming
  - it may be more cost-effective to put the day-to-day work out of house, while retaining strategic editorial control
- print costs can vary greatly depending on the format, paper size, type and weight, and the number of colours used
- paper costs are subject to substantial fluctuations

Timescales
- first issues usually take between one and two months to establish the format, design and content, as well as contact networks; thereafter frequencies can vary from weekly to quarterly

Activities
- research needs
- set objectives and editorial policy
- appoint editorial team, or select supplier if appropriate
- establish and test design and format
- outline content
- ideally, plan features and articles well in advance
  - keep flexibility to incorporate topical issues
- commission articles, photography and illustrations
- approve raw text
- lay out text, illustrations and photographs in a proof
- circulate proof copies for minor corrections and proof-reading
- circulate colour proof for final checking
- print and distribute

Feedback
- immediate feedback on the latest issue from people on the editorial teams or a sample group of readers
- readership surveys
- opinion surveys
- communication audit

Measurement
- effectiveness in achieving communication objectives
- reader appreciation
- retention of key messages

How to find out more

Editor's Handbook, British Association of Communicators in Business Ltd, 42 Borough High Street, London SE1 1XW 0171-378 7139

Creative Newspaper Design by Vic Giles and F. W. Hodgson, Heinemann, 1990

'Are house journals just hot air?' by Ian Spurr, *Involvement and Participation*, Autumn 1990

NEWSLETTERS

In contrast to newspapers and magazines, newsletters tend to be concerned with the exchange of more directly useful, factual information, like a portable bulletin board. They are an ideal medium for reaching small target groups, including site-specific audiences. They can provide support for internal newspapers, magazines or other media by enabling rapid updates under the same brand.

Strengths
- fast and immediate
- relatively cheap
- conveying short, focused bulletin-like material
- targeting specific audiences
- helping to reinforce the identity of the target group
  - for example service staff, team leaders or computer specialists
- strong on regular factual information
  - for example competitor analysis, new business won and so on

Opportunities
- give access and time to desktop publishing equipment, enabling groups to create their own newsletters, for example quality teams
- build in standard involvement mechanisms such as letters pages

Weaknesses
- budgets tend to rule out an 'editor' so it becomes a 'chore' for a volunteer or administrative support
- can look amateurish or cheap, especially if poorly laid out
- difficult to carry advanced graphical or photographic material without access to specialized equipment
- little opportunity to feature any subject in depth

Pitfalls
- deadlines can be missed and the newsletter can appear infrequently if no one has clear responsibility for it
  - damages credibility and loses readers
- messages undermined by poor editorial style or layout
  - this can be overcome by training in layout and editing

Budget issues
- can use existing word-processing equipment
- printing letterhead in advance to photocopy or laser-print on to

- if printing, producing camera-ready artwork, cost of litho-printing
- time spent in word-processing or desktop publishing material
- time spent on distribution

Timescales
- a basic newsletter can be created and photocopied onto branded paper almost immediately

Activities
- set objectives
- commissioning/writing material
- commissioning illustrations
- editing and sub-editing
- laying out pages
- finalizing approval
- proof-reading
- printing master copy
- photocopying
- distributing

Feedback
- return slips
  – comments box
- letters
- questionnaires/research
- correspondents' awaydays

Measurement
- measuring distribution of the newsletters
- retention of key messages
- level of participation

How to find out more
How to publish a Newsletter by Graham Jones, How To Books, 1994

British Association of Communicators in Business Ltd, 42 Borough High Street, London SE1 1XW 0171-378 7139

MANUALS, GUIDES AND HANDBOOKS

Manuals, guides and handbooks are often thought of as being very much the dusty, neglected corner of internal communication. But whose fault is that? Far too many are dull, incomprehensible and badly produced, and hardly ever 'sell' the actions people are supposed to take. If the 'leave the brains at the gate' culture still exists, it's in the world of the stuffy old manual.

There is a sense of false economy in that organizations will invest massively in a new process or a machine, but rush the job when it comes to producing the accompanying manuals, guides and handbooks that will put it all into action.

An attractive, well-written guide should pay for itself, as more people understand and feel committed to the actions they are expected to take, avoiding costly mistakes or inefficiency.

Strengths
- clear purpose
- familiar style and format
- informative and instructional
- provides a permanent record and reference
- forms the basis for training and quality procedures
- acts as arbiter in difficult situations
- screen versions are easily updated and accessible

Opportunities
- integrate messages into other media
  - for example put the messages of a manual in your organization's diary
  - run regular guides through newspapers and magazines
- link to an over-arching communication campaign
  - for example an awareness campaign to climax with the launch of the document
- use alongside multimedia
  - for example when training in a practical discipline, like correct lifting techniques, a multimedia programme could run a demonstration of how to do it, while the employees keep a handbook as their permanent record

– multimedia is becoming a strong format for on-line and disk-based guides (see multimedia, p. 98)
- revamp 'standard' media
  – the employee handbook, for example, can be more than just a dull collection of statutory information relating to contracts of employment; it can be a motivational, involving tool in its own right

Weaknesses
- perceived as dull and old-fashioned
- hard to mix motivational messages with instructions

Pitfalls
- written by experts . . .
  – many guides are put together by the people directly involved in the process they describe – too close to the process and the accompanying jargon
  – calling in someone from outside the project team to document the process can give valuable improvement lessons for the project itself, as a fresh mind may throw up new issues
  – in any event, drafts of the manuals need to be tested on the target audience for clarity and understanding
- over-documenting
  – many manuals and guides mushroom into huge indigestible tomes, thoroughly documenting the process, but completely intimidating the target audience

Budget issues
- scale of production, for example paper stock, binding and so on
- scale of research
  – to some extent driven by the needs of the target audience and the size of their document

Timescales
- three months from initial research through to produced documentation

Activities
- set objectives
- research the process
- produce and test outline against the document
- produce first draft, test against process and test with target audiences
- revise draft and test
- produce manual
- support with awareness-raising campaign if appropriate

Feedback	• have clear contact points printed in the documentation
Measurement	• effective implementation of the process • survey users before and after implementation
How to find out more	*How to write a Staff Manual* by S. L. Brock and S. R. Cabbell, Kogan Page, 1990

BROCHURES AND REPORTS

Brochures and reports are among the most highly finished of internal media, ranging from information about particular sites or products to employee versions of annual reports.

They can increase the credibility of the organization, and convey its values and key messages – even fairly complex ones like financial performance targets – through powerful combinations of text and graphics.

Strengths
- high quality
- high impact
- motivational
- opportunity for fine detail illustrations, design and photography
- gives the reader a personal copy, to take home, keep for reference or show to others
- readers can go at their own pace, re-reading to check understanding

Opportunities
- employee annual reports or business plans
  - adapted from the annual report, highlighting progress against performance targets
- useful for 'orientation' of potential, new or existing employees/suppliers

Weaknesses
- relatively high cost
- may date quickly

Pitfalls
- 'they spent how much on this?'
  - a glossy report may seem to some an expensive solution
- overdesigning
  - there can be a temptation to experiment with ever-more adventurous design in order to make the report stand out
  - the danger is that the visual effects will act against, rather than for, readability

Budget issues
- quality of production, for example paper stock, binding, number of colours and so on
- quantities produced, and likely 'shelf life', i.e. how many copies will you need to print over the predicted lifetime of the brochure or report?

Timescales	• a basic brochure could be generated in a month, but allow three months for a more sophisticated version
Activities	• set objectives • research the content • produce first draft • source illustrations, photographs and design • revise draft • lay approved text out in design • approve final proofs • print and distribute
Feedback	• contact points throughout brochures and reports • tear-off slips for replies or requests for information
Measurement	• retention of key messages • survey to gauge audience reaction
How to find out more	*How to communicate your Message: the PICKUP guide to promotion* by David Carter and Paul Stirner, HMSO, 1993

BRIEFING PACKS

Briefing packs are the foundation of successful team briefings (see team briefing, p. 10). A core brief sent out from the centre can help ensure that key messages are delivered in a consistent and timely (even simultaneous) way, right across the organization.

Strengths
- makes life easier for the briefer by providing the core information and giving guidance on running the briefing
- makes delivery of information consistent
- gives the centre greater control over what information is shared, and how
- providing the briefing system is settled, packs can be created and distributed to briefers in a matter of minutes via fax or e-mail
- allows use of the full range of media, depending on resource and need, in conjunction with face-to-face techniques
- relatively simple to measure effectiveness and spot gaps

Opportunities
- different levels of pack can be created depending on need, for example for communication of major restructuring, regional managers may pass on detailed lists, first line managers may use video or a desktop presenter, individuals may receive their own pack
- dedicated packs can be created for briefings that need to be repeated for different groups over time, introducing a particular process or product: these can become quite sophisticated, using audio-visual materials, booklets and so on
- local input into a centralized brief
  - ideally only part of the brief should include mandatory messages from the centre that must be covered: the rest of the agenda can therefore be driven by local needs in selecting optional messages or covering topics of local interest
- customization of messages
  - the system can be flexible enough for briefers to interpret and package messages in a way right and relevant for their audience
- agenda setting by teams
  - teams across the organization can be encouraged to

put forward their ideas for subjects to be covered in
the team briefing
- prepared answers to likely questions
  - briefers can use guidelines on how to answer
    questions likely to arise from particular topics

Weaknesses
- relies on the skill – and goodwill – of briefers to use
  the pack effectively
- producing a full set of documentation can be slow and
  time-consuming
- briefers can rely too closely on the core briefing packs,
  failing to customize the briefing for their own team

Pitfalls
- information overload or underload
  - hitting the right degree of emphasis on specific topics
    requires careful thought and consultation, for
    example by setting up a sample group of briefers to
    help identify which topics need to be covered, and
    in what detail
- no news
  - because of cycles in the organization's work, it may
    be that briefings may be overloaded with information
    in some periods, quiet at others: keeping to a regular
    format, for example including regular progress
    reports, will help ensure that there is always
    something tangible to report on, and planning
    ahead will help to minimize any imbalances in the
    amount of material available
- misunderstanding
  - briefers may be using the packs with little
    preparation, and need to be able to grasp the key
    messages as quickly as possible, without the danger
    of ambiguity or misunderstanding
- patronizing instructions
  - the centre may be so keen on consistency that instead
    of guidelines, the briefing pack gives over-detailed
    and restrictive instructions on how to run the briefing
- domination by the centre
  - because the centre produces the packs there may be
    a danger of the agenda being skewed towards
    Head Office life, and not adequately reflecting the
    needs and interest of employees as a whole
  - the briefings need to be flexible enough to
    incorporate a large proportion of material of purely
    local interest
- prioritizing the pack over the process
  - producing well-presented briefing packs will have

little impact if the cascade process itself is flawed,
or if briefers lack the skill and the confidence to run
a briefing

Budget issues
- time of briefer, team and people monitoring the success of the briefing
- pack production and distribution costs

Timescales
- virtually immediate for urgent briefing packs
- plan main topics up to three months in advance for monthly briefs, include subsidiary topics up to a week in advance and keep a 'stop press' sheet to be inserted for any last minute additions

Activities
- determine key messages
- research local environment
- identify best format for the briefing pack
- prioritize the messages, allocating time for them at the briefing
- structure the briefing, aiming to give interest and variety, while covering the key messages in appropriate depth
- draft the briefing pack, creating any supporting visuals or documents
- edit the packs and win approval
- circulate the packs
- monitor performance

Feedback
- build feedback route into the briefing itself
- include specific questions where the briefer needs to report back on the team's views
- include space in the pack to record comments, ideas and actions arising from each point of the briefing, and include a summary action plan format to capture actions and responsibilities arising from the meeting

Measurement
- gather briefer's reactions to the pack and ideas for improvement
- measure the success of the briefings themselves
  - for example did the briefing take place by the deadline?
  - for example how well were key messages understood by the target audience?

How to find out more
- most materials on team briefing will contain guidance on pack preparation

4 Electronic communication

Fixed and mobile telephones, voicemail,
audiotex and answerphones
Fax
Audiotape
Audioconferencing
Moving light screens
Video
Videoconferencing and videophones
Videotext
Internal TV systems
Direct Broadcast by Satellite (DBS)
Time-shift broadcast

FIXED AND MOBILE TELEPHONES, VOICE MAIL, AUDIOTEX AND ANSWERPHONES

The increase in the number of direct telephone lines has led to most of us becoming more and more accessible to phone calls, as technology advances have made it possible to bypass switchboards and secretaries.

Organizations have taken longer to adapt to the resulting changes, for example in failing to encourage colleagues to answer each other's phones. Instead, more technological solutions are on the way. For example most networked systems now let you divert calls from one handset to another or to a shared answerphone. More sophisticated voice mail installations allow individuals extensive control of their own telephone environment via a host of newer facilities, such as customizing outgoing messages, diverting to numbers outside the system, and remote message collection and handling.

Mobile phones add yet another dimension, revolutionizing people's ability to stay in touch (for example when travelling). The latest models and network improvements include dialling from extensive stored address books, missed call recording and even the ability to make e-mail connections from a laptop PC.

Most mobile phone users, thanks to the call diversion technologies available on digital networks, can already divert their calls seamlessly to another number, with no inconvenience to their callers. However, the industry is working towards complete number portability. It's now possible to buy one telephone number which will cover all your telecommunication devices, whether it's your mobile phone, your pager, your fixed phone, your mobile laptop or fax.

Meanwhile, new applications are constantly being found for techniques like audiotex, usually used to present a menu of short recorded messages to callers, allowing them to select the option they want using a tone phone. Such techniques are increasingly being used to support information hotlines, say for pensions and benefits information, and more recently for interactive services that allow an employee to register preferences or lodge a request.

Communication professionals who want to make sure that the organization is communicating effectively, internally and externally, have to step outside their conventional 'box' of responsibility and review whether the right mix of hardware, software and telephone skills training is available.

Continued advances along these lines can make not just the choice of options but the evaluation of benefits a bewildering process. Well aware of the problem, the industry is more than willing to talk through how the technological solutions can meet your needs. However, as with all media buying, the best defence against making expensive mistakes is to have your objectives clearly set out first before talking to the 'experts'.

The kind of issue to look out for is where new facilities are regarded by the organization as 'perks' rather than business tools. This happened with mobile phones, for example, which were often allocated on the basis of seniority – and often therefore to deskbound people – rather than being targeted at people who could use a mobile to best effect on the company's behalf.

Strengths
- telephone personal, immediate and interactive with the ability on both sides to ask questions and check understanding
- now increasingly mobile, phones make use of dead time, such as when travelling
- allows shorter, more informal messages, simpler requests
- confirming arrangements, reaching agreement
- telephone useful for 'off the record' or casual conversations
- big advantage of voice mail is that you can effectively 'broadcast' the messages to a number of people
  - for example making sure that a management team handles a crisis in a consistent way
  - this is especially useful for urgent communication when dealing across time zones
- audiotex/voice recognition techniques are a cost-

effective way of giving callers a range of possible information/request options from one telephone number

- audiotex, answerphones and voice mail offer callers an instant response when no one is available to take calls

Opportunities
- set and monitor standards for all telephone behaviour including answering, message-taking and message-leaving to ensure consistency of quality
- offer opportunities to develop telephone skills, for example learning how to summarize to edge conversations gently to a close
- tailor different combinations of services to different audiences
- targeted messages via audiotex
  - keep recorded messages short, a maximum of two minutes, and where possible break into short segments
  - update the messages frequently, so there's an urge to 'keep up with the news'
  - tone phones mean that you can select certain options offered you, tapping into different information
  - you can program some systems to generate call data, judging the relative demand and profiling people who call for particular services
- vote lines
  - telephone logging numbers to record how many people favour a particular course of action
  - for example choosing which charity should benefit from next year's social responsibility fund

Weaknesses
- a lack of control, with the possibility of time-wasting and distractions at either end
- relies on notemaking for a record
- messages can become vague without visual stimulation
- with ordinary telephone calling you choose a good time for *you* to make the call, but it may not be the right time for the receiver
- despite familiarity with answerphones, many people still have great difficulty leaving a coherent message on one, largely because callers are geared up for interaction
- audiotex and helplines rely on the motivation of people to call them
- audiotex options rely on the wide availability of tone phones

Pitfalls
- creating opportunities to indulge in small talk and 'social grazing' by phone
- one side forgetting that they may have more information in front of them than the other
  - check the other understands
- believing that the phone is quicker than writing, when for complex tasks the fax may be more time-effective
  - for example talking through corrections to a long report, when it would be far easier and clearer to mark the changes to the report itself
- feeding information through in a disorganized way
  - telephone conversations can be unstructured with distracting ideas popping out at random
- people can fail to see the need to prepare for a conversation, in the way that they would with written communication
- compelling receiver to make notes
  - even shorthand experts have a hard time keeping up with phone conversations, because natural speech contains blind alleys and confusions
- 'mechanical' answerphone and audiotex messages
  - people are less likely to use these services if the message greeting them sounds like an officious android
- endless audiotex options
  - while the virtue of a flexible audiotex system is that you can offer many options to callers, the more you list the more confused callers will be as they wait for the option closest to their need

Budget issues
- telephone usage is getting easier to monitor through improved management information systems, which means choosing the best telephone option is becoming an increasingly complex decision
  - draw up a short list of your top three suppliers and set your selection criteria
- for voice mail, you may need a cost-benefit analysis on the basis of equipment hire or purchase vs time-savings and boosted efficiency

Timescales
- for big telecommunication changes, spend at least a month researching the field
- demand fast delivery and installation from the time you place your order
- once established, all these media can be used immediately, and are easy to update

Activities
- research needs and set objectives
- research solutions
  - hardware, software and training
- install communication systems
- monitor use
- look for training gaps and target training on improving performance
- monitor telecommunication press for details on new products and services

Feedback
- where recording systems are available, invite callers to leave their comments
- offer helplines, access lines, and list telephone numbers in all relevant documentation, improving accessibility

Measurement
- number of times audiotex, voice mail and answerphones are used

How to find out more
- talk to telephone companies

Telephone Skills by Maria Pemberton, Industrial Society Press, 1988

Quality Calls: making the most of the phone (video-based open learning), The Industrial Society, 1995

FAX

Fax machines are now an essential and expected item for organizations of all sizes. Newer models may be integrated with phones, answerphones or personal computers, and use standard (as opposed to photo-sensitive) paper.

Strengths
- direct, clear and immediate
- now that paper-based faxes and faxes linked to laser printers are becoming more widespread there is little difference in look and feel from a letter
  - short faxes may be cheaper than post
- leaves sender and receiver a written record
- a multi-fax system can send one fax to a range of destinations virtually simultaneously
- international communication
  - a cost-effective way of communicating across time zones
- fax systems can receive e-mail and electronic faxes from desk-based and laptop computers (e.g. Applefax)
- 'brands' each fax page with your identity across the top
- some laser printers can now serve computing and fax needs
- more home use means that flexible working becomes increasingly possible, including to overcome short-time crises like rail strikes

Opportunities
- grade your faxes
  - introduce an 'urgency' grading system
- the fax ident is an opportunity to brand your communication
  - if your fax automatically codes the time sent, ensure that you update the clock in line with time changes
- introduce dedicated fax lines
  - maximize access and interactivity, and speed up receipt and attention
- cover during down time
  - to ensure constant access, consider diverting your fax automatically, when it is engaged or being maintained
- fax newsletters
  - immediate updates to keep in touch with satellite offices, or people who work from home

- fax information services
  - faxing out information on request
  - some organizations link this to a system that recognizes tone phones and computer services; the callers press for the relevant option from a menu and the specific information sheet is faxed to them
  - you can use this discretely to 'market' your own services
- fax briefings
  - support team briefing by using fax to distribute the core briefs, enabling last minute 'stop press' items

Weaknesses
- having a fax exposes you to junk-faxes
  - you pay in wasted fax paper for other people's marketing, so avoid having your number published in a fax directory, unless you have an overriding reason for doing so; consider a fax-barring system that will only accept faxes from recognized numbers
- black and white only
- poor, slow and costly photo reproduction
  - newer machines are getting better at handling photographs and fine illustrations, but older machines are not good at handling faxes with large shaded areas, for example text and photographs on dark coloured papers
- time wasted in recalling, checking arrival, resending

Pitfalls
- speed scrawl
  - people tend to handwrite them at speed
- permanently engaged
  - because large organizations do not adequately invest in fax machines, many fax lines are jammed solid, wasting time as senders pile their documents in queues waiting for the line to be freed
  - some phone systems enable an automatic divert to another machine if the line is engaged
- losing fax
  - relying on the internal post to circulate faxes can be a little dangerous
  - the curly fax paper has an alarming habit of creeping down the back of the fax machine, out of sight – a fax 'catcher' should help to minimize this problem
- out of sight, out of mind
  - given the logistical problems and opportunities for error with faxes, surprisingly few people take the service-minded step of ringing to check that their fax

has arrived – if nothing else this step will draw
attention to your fax
- because 'faxing' is the 'easy' last stage of producing
a document, and relies only on a number, people can
quite happily send faxes to the wrong destination,
wasting time and causing embarrassment
- jam today, jam tomorrow
  - fax jams are still common and particularly frustrating
  in the case of long documents
  - consider faxing in segments – it may cost more in
  fax header sheets, but it makes the document more
  digestible all round
- the ident 'giveaway'
  - people sometimes forget how much is revealed by
  the fax ident
  - fudging a missed deadline? – your ident may carry
  the correct time (unless of course you reset the
  clock in your favour)
  - seamless subcontracting? – if your internal or
  external customer is unaware that you've
  subcontracted the work, they will soon realize when
  thy see someone else's fax ident
- the 'idiot'-proof fax
  - deciding which machines to buy or hire rests on the
  balance of functionality vs usability – some fax
  machines offer barely used features that simply
  confuse users
  - few organizations bother to train employees how to
  use features on fax machines, for example clocking
  up wasted hours as people laboriously tap in the last
  number, when they could use the redial button
  - common sense is not that common, as you realize
  when you receive a blank fax because the person
  at the other end has put their work wrong-side down
  on their fax machine
- *'more than my job's worth to touch that machine'*
  - most fax machines suffer much abuse, and even the
  most basic maintenance is rarely carried out; the
  result is that organizations will habitually send out
  dirty faxes, without knowing it, until a horrified
  executive finally sees the illegible mess that the client
  received
  - keeping the fax clean also helps to prevent jams and
  breakdowns, but most of all gives a clearer copy to the
  receiver
  - some faxes react badly to the common practice of

pencilling the fax number to call on the back of the first page – it can rub off as the paper passes through the roller, sprinkling graphite around the machine

Budget issues
- assess the hire vs buy decision
- consider upgrading to paper-based fax by comparing the real cost of photocopying floppy, fading documents
- rather like the movement from mainframes to personal computers, it could make sense for many organizations to move from high capacity centralized faxes to decentralized simpler faxes, spread across the organization, saving people's time

Timescales
- in theory, faxing direct from your computer screen to another computer screen is almost immediate
- at the other end of the timescale, writing, printing and sending a fax to many areas of Eastern Europe, for example, will give you much time for reflection and practice with the redial button – the only saving grace being that the postal service there is equally unreliable

Activities
- set objectives and plan
- research needs, volumes and types of faxes sent
- research fax solutions
- site fax machines and monitor usage and quality of faxes sent

Feedback
- build in a reply section to any communication sent

Measurement
- check fax quality by testing both with customers and with internal fax machines
- usage from fax/telephone bills
- examine *how* people are writing faxes
  - time taken to generate and send vs alternative methods such as phone

How to find out more
- Talk to telecommunication/equipment suppliers

AUDIOTAPE

An almost universal medium, audiotape is well established for internal communication uses such as magazine programmes and open learning. It's familiar, relatively cheap and, if carefully produced, can personalize and bring issues alive that would die on the printed page. Newer CD-audio and DVD (Digital Versatile Disk) systems allow higher quality recording and more stable media. With Minidisc/DVD, it's possible to edit the audio material to target groups or even individuals.

Strengths
- intimate, direct and personal
- personalizes and dramatizes issues, which makes it ideal for motivational speeches, debate and demonstrating personal commitment
- people listen in their own 'dead' time, at their own pace, for example when commuting to work
- high perceived value; people are less likely to throw cassettes away than paper communication
- almost as flexible as print, and more personalized
- cost-effective for reaching large numbers of dispersed audiences
    - for example sales forces
- one-off events
    - for example distributing a short motivational, personal speech from top management in times of crisis
- small and convenient for portability
- can reach anyone worldwide with access to a cassette-recorder
    - audio-cassette mailing fast and cheap

Opportunities
- invite listener comment and let them set the agenda
- feature listeners heavily in the recorded features
- take comments from a dedicated answerphone or phone line
- support or follow up with documentation to carry any detailed information
    - for example the tape could carry the motivational 'end of year' message from the management team, while the accompanying document lays out the facts and figures
    - alternatively, interweave the structure of the tape and

the document, cross-referencing between the two, as in traditional open-learning packages
- in line with equal opportunities it's also a cost-effective way of recruiting and informing visually handicapped people.

Weaknesses
- poor at conveying complex information, because listeners cannot take it in without visual stimuli, and cannot 'read' at their own pace
- difficult to 'browse' through
- unit cost typically higher than parallel print documents
- could be seen as poor relation to video

Pitfalls
- danger of producing tape programmes that:
  - sound as if they use 'written' rather than spoken English
  - have an unclear structure
  - have long, unbroken items
  - are longer than the audience's average commuting distance
- can damage management credibility if their performance is poor or overtly propagandist

Budget issues
- low-budget programmes can be turned round rapidly in-house by using a high-speed copier (only practical for audiences smaller than 20)
- if you are aiming for a professional-sounding result, in most cases it will make sense to get tenders and creative proposals from audio producers, removing the need for you to budget for initial equipment such as recorder, microphone, headphones, (plus mixer and editing deck if not editing in a studio)
- in any event, producing audiotapes takes a great deal of project management time
- other likely costs include:
  - studio hire including engineer/editor
  - bulk copying
  - printing on to the cassettes (on-body printing)
  - printing an inlay card to go in the cassette box
  - distribution costs

Timescales
- almost immediate for a simple programme, edited and bulk duplicated on your own equipment, for example recording a chairman's address for circulation
- at least six weeks for planning, producing and circulating a basic 20-minute magazine programme

Activities
- set objectives
- set and agree content
- set up and record interviews/reports/footage
- arrange for scripts and inlay card to be written
- arrange for inlay card to be designed
- win approval of scripts and footage
  - circulate transcripts of the quotes to be used if necessary
- produce any supporting documentation or inlay card
- record presenter's script
- edit master tape
  - cut the recorded footage together with any scripted recording, musical stings, etc.
  - cut the final tape to target length
  - win approval for edit if necessary
- bulk copy cassettes
- distribute cassettes

Feedback
- listeners can record messages/comments on tape and return

Measurement
- survey to measure retention of key messages, understanding of issues

How to find out more
- contact internal communication agencies for production consultancy

AUDIOCONFERENCING

Anyone with a telephone can set up an audioconference from their desk. Most modern telephone exchanges and telephone companies offer conferencing facilities.

There are also specialist devices and companies available to help you link together groups of people sitting at tables around special audioconference microphones. Like a real conference, groups can be split into seminars, reconvened, split into other groups – regardless of where they are in the world.

Strengths
- cost-effective way of linking groups of people across the world
- used to bring together any group of people you need to have a meeting with where time or travel costs may be an issue
- relatively quick and easy to set up, depending on the number of participants and the technology used

Opportunities
- record the conference, circulating it to absentees
- digital switching means that the equipment can switch faster from speaker to speaker, improving interactivity
- circulate the agenda and any other vital reference documents in advance to help structure the conversation

Weaknesses
- needs careful management to ensure one party or group is not dominating the meeting
- takes time to get used to audioconferencing etiquette – for example identifying yourself before you speak
- impossible to monitor participants' activity
- requires visual support for interest and to convey detailed information
- seen as a poor relation to videoconferencing
- relies on variable line quality worldwide

Pitfalls
- temptation to patch in too many lines, reducing participation

Budget issues
- most modern business telephone systems allow you to combine two or more internal lines with an external call
- three-way calling is available on modern digital telephone exchanges, enabling you to combine two

external lines with your own, if you have the symbols # and * on your telephone
- hiring specialists to manage the conference for you
- investing in audioconferencing equipment

Timescales
- almost immediate if arranging a small conference call from your own phone

Activities
- set objectives
- agree meeting time and circulate agenda
- explain the ground rules of audioconferencing to anyone new to the technique
- distribute any visuals or documents that will be needed
- organize any additional equipment, for example whiteboards that can 'fax' their images
- call participants and welcome them individually to the conference
- manage the audioconference, cueing in participants and ensuring that no one is dominating the event

Feedback
- gather feedback as people 'leave' the conference
- fax 'happy sheets' to survey immediate reactions

Measurement
- cost-benefit analysis vs travel time

How to find out more
- check instructions on your phone system for the ability to conference call
- talk to your telephone company
- talk to specialist audioconferencing companies

MOVING LIGHT SCREENS

Moving light screens vary in size from the vast screens used at football events and pop concerts to the 'running strips' used in shops, stations and reception areas. An echo of Times Square, they still have enough novelty to conjure up the image of romance and urgency, of dealing rooms and journalistic scoops.

In reality, the 'news' carried on moving light screens is much more mundane, but organizations are beginning to find that this is a powerful way to convey short messages, from the organization's latest share price to the number of calls handled by a department, from sales to date to performance against target.

Strengths
- immediacy, acting as a constant 'bush telegraph'
- regular update on a standard range of information
  - for example key performance indicators, cost savings made
  - for example the winners of regular competitions
- silent medium
- clear, updatable public display
- simultaneous 'broadcast' to multiple sites
- no distraction
  - people glance at it in their own time

Opportunities
- the modern equivalent of welcome boards – being able to customize messages in reception, for example people's names
- listing the events happening across the organization today
- tie in with external databases
  - use the system to display key information
  - for example stock market news on related organizations
- competition news
  - news headlines about related or competing organizations
- reinforcing culture
  - for example running the mission statement on a rolling basis, to remind the audience

Weaknesses
- can carry only brief, simple messages
- only referred to for short periods

- a fairly passive medium, relying on 'casual' interest in dead time
- will become moving wallpaper, ignored by the audience, if the information is not kept fresh and interesting
- it is difficult to distinguish urgent messages from the routine
- even with today's technology, not very readable
- needs a fairly large display area, and careful consideration needs to be given to sightlines and the surrounding interior design
- the movement can be irritating if viewed all day from a peripheral position

Pitfalls
- yesterday's news
  - often the information is not updated, because it is considered a low priority task
  - the whole point of the system is that it is *immediate*, there are more effective ways of conveying routine information
- long sentences
  - consider the speed of character movement for readability and understanding
- font mania
  - making the text less readable by pushing the font functions to the limit

Budget issues
- hire vs buy decision on equipment
- installation and maintenance
- licensing of any external data used
- time spent producing and updating text

Timescales
- once established, updating messages should be almost immediate

Activities
- set objectives
- draft text
- edit text to readable length
- where possible and appropriate, adjust speed and pause times
- test text – checking that it is readable by the target audience
- approve text
- put text on-screen

Feedback
- response to on-screen requests, for example publicizing a telephone number to call with feedback

Measurement
- survey to measure retention of messages
- study to identify how quickly and widely the messages spread, and the routes they follow

How to find out more
- research moving light screen suppliers and compare products

VIDEO

The increased reliability and availability of video has made it an essential medium, supplanting temperamental and fiddly media like film, film strips and slide-tape packages. Ranging from low cost training videos to broadcast-standard production, video is a flexible medium. The spread of camcorders has made in-house video filming possible and the development of accessible digital recording means intermediate users can edit and manipulate video-imagery without the need for expert training. Professional video-editing services can still add considerable value, however, and are worth checking out if you want a slick finished product or a more creative approach.

For most organizations, producing a full-scale corporate video is a rite of passage that brings credibility and status. Consequently, many organizations produce corporate videos with vague objectives, in the belief that they *ought* to have one. Many corporate videos are expensive, glossy and call on the latest video graphics and presentation techniques, others are more limited. The beauty is that the style chosen reflects the culture, and more than with most media, you can show rather than say.

Strengths
- high impact, good at conveying emotion
- immediate and direct
- gives a holistic view of the organization: locations, people, products, services, processes, actions
- excellent for training demonstrations
- can reach anyone with access to a video-recorder

Opportunities
- regular video magazine programmes
- support with documents to carry complicated detail
- build in comment slots to magazine programmes
  - people film reports/pieces to camera on their own camcorder, or one loaned by the organization
- 'owned by employees'
  - employees may buy in to a video if the concept, ideas and presentation involve them
  - this also legitimizes looking a little low-budget – if Carol of finance is doing the presenting, the

expectation is that this is not going to be of broadcast standard

Weaknesses
- poor at conveying complex information
- easy to look amateurish
- people tend to expect broadcast quality
- relatively high cost
- difficulty in scheduling 'viewing' periods
- short shelf life
- a linear medium, making it difficult to find specific material (contrast with the video content of multimedia)

Pitfalls
- using too many video gimmicks which can get in the way of the message
- all things to all people
  - corporate videos tend to be used for a variety of purposes, from sales to education links, from lobbying to induction, which means that they can end up rather bland
  - there is also the danger that one key audience will be put off, for example using a 'salesy' corporate video for graduate recruitment
  - consider edited options for different purposes

Budget issues
- project management time
- equipment purchase/hire
- fees of scriptwriter, director and camera crew if appropriate
- editing fees
- video stock
- duplication, packaging and distribution

Timescales
- allow at least a month for basic video production

Activities
- set objectives
- plan
- produce a script outline
- approve outline
  - take into account logistics, for example there is no point suggesting multiple locations if the budget will only run to filming at one site
- produce full script
- approve script
- produce any supporting documentation
- hire director and camera crew and explain what you are trying to achieve
- organize filming, minimizing disruption

- off-line editing
  - create a rough version of the programme to make sure that the proposed edits work and send the right message
- on-line editing
  - extremely expensive, building up a master tape by laying down material in sequence
  - extensive editing can add greatly to the budget
- duplicating master

Feedback
- print contact name/number on the video package
- survey for target audience's reactions

Measurement
- retention of key messages and understanding of key issues
- audience appreciation

How to find out more

Using Television and Video in Business by Andrew Crofts, Mercury, 1991

Interactivity: designing and using interactive video by M. Picciotto, I. Robertson and R. Colley, Kogan Page, 1989

Interactive Media: the human issues by Richard Tucker, Kogan Page, 1989

International Visual Communications Association (IVCA), 2nd Floor, Bolsover House, 5/6 Clipstone St, London W1P 8LD 0171-580 0962

VIDEOCONFERENCING AND VIDEOPHONES

Advances in telecommunication technologies and the spread of fibre optic networks and digital exchanges have made videotelephony more of an affordable reality. Dedicated videoconferencing units are being used by more organizations as reliability improves and costs fall.

Already on the market, but not yet in widespread use, is digital video, which allows PC users to link up for conferences and presentations over the Internet. Supporting material can be sent to participants simultaneously with the conference link in electronic format.

Strengths
- meetings between small groups worldwide without incurring travel costs
- minimal travel time
- bridge-building across geographical and language barriers
- enables speedier decision-making

Opportunities
- video-record conference for reference, or to circulate to non-participants
- carefully 'chair' conference to ensure full participation
- involve and unite different sites or cultures, for example two companies preparing for a merger or two research departments collaborating on a task
- circulate documents and samples in advance, to save over-reliance on viewing via the camera
- use extra cameras to transmit illustrations, for example a camera dedicated to slides

Weaknesses
- still relatively costly
- not quite as good as face-to-face contact
- poor understanding of teleconferencing 'etiquette' can create a chaotic atmosphere
- need to wait for a critical mass of compatible videoconferencing units or high-quality videophones, enabling wider use and greater familiarity
- video quality on videophones currently fairly poor
- timeslots are expensive
  - promptness is sometimes a problem

Pitfalls	• can be seen as 'gimmicky'
	• over-reliance, or inappropriate use
	  – there is no substitute for face-to-face meetings in terms of building and maintaining relationships
	  – just as you would probably not feel comfortable employing or buying from someone you had only 'interviewed' by videoconference, they would not feel that they had met you properly either
	• out of sight, out of mind
	  – some people take the need to be at a meeting less seriously because it's local
	• time zone insomnia
	  – the fact that members of distant videoconferences save travel time and money is significant, but it still may leave one group working in the middle of the night

Budget issues	• videoconferencing suites available for hire in many large towns • videoconferencing hardware dropping in price • low cost one-to-one videoconferencing increasing through use of videophones and PCs
Timescales	• the only limitations are the availability of equipment and of the people involved in the meeting
Activities	• set objectives • research potential suppliers • hire vs buy decision about whether to install suites or hire facilities • raise awareness of videoconferencing and offer training
Feedback	• instant feedback at meeting
Measurement	• cost-benefit analysis vs travel time
How to find out more	*Using Television and Video in Business* by Andrew Crofts, Mercury, 1991 International Visual Communications Association (IVCA), 2nd Floor, Bolsover House, 5/6 Clipstone St, London W1P 8LD 0171-580 0962

VIDEOTEXT

Many organizations are now running in-house videotext service, like the screen-based services offered by television broadcasters such as CEEFAX, ORACLE and 4-TEL.

With screens scattered throughout the organization, text can be updated almost instantaneously. Using a rolling format, one page moves automatically to the next after a set time. The sequence of pages repeats until updates are made.

Strengths
- 'high-tech' appearance
- can be updated immediately
  - for example to make an 'announcement' to employees
- particularly useful in organizations with a high public profile where there is a need to conveys news to an internal audience before the media does
- provides clear text summaries, reaching everyone in public areas
- can reach scattered sites in continental Europe and worldwide
- uses TV sets which can also be used for other purposes

Opportunities
- reach all parts of the organization simultaneously
- 'free screen'
  - boost involvement in the medium by throwing over some of the pages to employees
- makes use of the grapevine – the 'did you see?' syndrome

Weaknesses
- relies on the target audience to have the time and feel motivated to read the pages
- not everyone may have equal access to the text screens

Pitfalls
- *plus ça change . . .*
  - there may be little to fill the text pages, resulting in the same pages appearing with monotonous frequency, or the same page staying on screen *ad infinitum*
- yesterday's news
  - often the information is not updated, because it is considered a low priority task, while the whole point of the system is that it is urgent
- danger, artist at work

- there may be a temptation to create a graphic impact with what is essentially a text-based system – very hard to pull off successfully
- the graphic support, rather like crude typewriter pictures, added to which you have a limited range of colours and the results can be crude and garish
- worst of all, selecting background colours that make the text hard to read
- *'got a screen to fill'*
  - overloading the screen with too much text or too many graphics, making it unreadable
- *'any idiot can write on a screen'*
  - as a public medium, with few of the audience doing more than glance at the screen, the text needs to grab the reader and convey its message instantly
  - professional writing skills will enhance the retention of key messages, producing shorter, 'snappier' text

Budget issues
- after initial start up, relatively easy to maintain, with comparatively low running costs

Timescales
- 'pages' can be updated almost instantly from a computer keyboard

Activities
- set objectives
- design the overall 'rolling format' of pages
- decide who will draft text for the pages
- create a system for approving text

Feedback
- touch-screen technology can increase the interactive element of videotext and internal television, producing a limited intranet system that can be accessed by employees and customers alike
- review content and reactions with a sample group taken from the target audience

Measurement
- awareness and use of the medium
  - for example how often a day someone reads the screen
- retention of key messages

How to find out more
- research sites, existing or potential
- research human resources, for example existing editors
- research information needed

INTERNAL TV SYSTEMS

Internal TV systems can be used to run a schedule of internal programmes throughout the day, or at specified viewing hours. Overplayed, this can have something of a 'big brother' feel, with all the TV monitors on-site showing pictures of happy workers, or handing down corporate messages.

However, it is particularly useful for multi-site and multinational organizations, which need to reach everyone at once with consistent messages, and to break down barriers between people at different locations (see the following section on Direct Broadcast by Satellite). It can also be used in foyers for visitors and for live broadcasts of annual general meetings to remote shareholder groups.

Strengths
- familiar, popular medium
- high impact
- programmes easy and quick to digest
- immediacy
- showing locations, actions, processes

Opportunities
- possibility of live two-way television
- video or telephone links to bring in questions or input from other sites
- training, product demonstrations
- branch networks

Weaknesses
- as with any other TV station, the broadcast hours are expensive to fill
- could be perceived as a luxury at times of cost-cutting
- can have a 'big brother' feel
  - in some systems even the volume is fixed so that the TV cannot be turned down
- can distract people when they should be doing other things
- 'watch with mother' – the only way you can be sure people are watching is to sit down with them and watch the programme
- it's hard to match broadcast quality, so your version can appear rather amateurish to the audience
  - in terms of picture quality, production values and presenter style

Pitfalls
- 'voice of god' propaganda
  - internal TV should not be an ego-trip for senior managers, neither should it be too overtly biased to management messages
  - the TV audience is sophisticated and can spot items that look unbalanced
  - if you've chosen to take a fairly independent stance in your programming, you stand the risk of losing management support
- talking heads
  - because of logistics and costs, internal TV programmes often rely on long, staged interviews with senior managers, which can become sterile
  - worse, some dispense with the interview and have the manager talking direct to camera, difficult to do unless the manager is well trained
  - many interviews are poorly edited, but the edit points in an interview are actually a good opportunity to 'cut away' to footage or stills of real things to liven up the programme
  - even abstract concepts like quality have a physical or human dimension to illustrate them, for example performance measures or simply shots of people working

Budget issues
- large initial investment in equipment
- large production budget needed to feed the system with regular programming

Timescales
- most programmes will take three months to produce
- when programmes are off-air, the screens can be used to carry text (see videotext, p. 81)

Activities
- set objectives
- commission and plan programmes (see video, p. 76)

Feedback
- feedback at live events
- audience surveys

Measurement
- retention of key messages

How to find out more

Using Television and Video in Business by Andrew Crofts, Mercury, 1991

International Visual Communications Association (IVCA), 2nd Floor, Bolsover House, 5/6 Clipstone St, London W1P 8LD 0171-580 0962

DIRECT BROADCAST BY SATELLITE (DBS)

Satellite technology can encode and broadcast live or recorded programmes, direct to an organization. You can use this as a fast way of distributing video magazine programmes around multiple sites, with each site recording the signal on a video-recorder at a pre-arranged time.

You can also link live events happening across different locations, for example drawing together a network of stores for a sales launch, or enabling your chief executive to talk simultaneously to everyone at all sites.

Strengths
- high impact
- high potential for interactivity
- carries the kudos of live TV
  - it is still unusual, and impresses audiences
- emotional and motivational
- reaches an entire audience at one go
  - has the unifying effect of a nationwide event
  - circumvents the grapevine because everyone experiences the same material simultaneously
- instant distribution
  - no delay or uncertainty waiting for tapes to arrive
- reaches audiences at geographically diverse sites within the satellite's footprint
- encryption helps to prevent security breaches

Opportunities
- schedule in input from remote locations
- 'low cost' live input by viewers telephoning in questions to the presenter
- use for one-off events, such as merger announcements, product launches
- interactive training
  - questions relayed live by telephone to a central trainer

Weaknesses
- high cost
- poor on complicated, factual messages
- technologically complex, especially linking live sites together
- requires basic equipment at all sites (dish, decoder, video-recorder)

Pitfalls	• cost may outweigh benefit of immediacy • more cost-effective broadcast mechanisms may be available (see the following section on time-shift broadcast) • *'we borrowed Eurovision's satellite'* – live video and audio feeds from remote locations are technically difficult to pull off and, rather like the Eurovision song contest, may leave your presenter beached with no one to talk to
Budget issues	• may be cost-effective if it replaces cost of regional conferences and roadshows • filming video material including number of locations • renting or buying equipment, for example receiving (downlink) dishes • live or recorded? • number of locations to link 'live' • equipment and transmission costs • outside expertise and production • down time as staff watch the programmes
Timescales	• most events and programmes need at least three months' planning • emergency live broadcasts can be arranged quickly
Activities	• set objectives, outline plan and target timescale • invite proposals from DBS specialists • select proposal and review • script and plan out event in detail • book satellite time • organize equipment, film crews, presenters • organize satellite uplink from any sites sending equipment for broadcast • rehearse event, especially any input from remote locations • run the event
Feedback	• instant feedback on day • ongoing audience reaction survey
Measurement	• survey to measure retention of key messages
How to find out more	*Using Television and Video in Business* by Andrew Crofts, Mercury, 1991 International Visual Communications Association (IVCA), 2nd Floor, Bolsover House, 5/6 Clipstone St, London W1P 8LD 0171-580 0962

TIME-SHIFT BROADCAST

Because most people now have video-recorders, there's
an opportunity for organizations to transmit programmes
for their target audiences to record off-air. For example
the BBC can transmit programmes in the early hours
of the morning, using the frequencies used by BBC1 and
BBC2. The target audience simply set their video-
recorders, and watch the material when *they* want.

Strengths
- kudos and near-immediacy of broadcast TV
- reaching home-based audiences over a familiar and
  trusted medium
- can be a low cost method of distributing video material
- audience views at its own pace and convenience
- audience does not need to set a new channel on its
  video-recorders

Opportunities
- showcasing important events, such as organizational
  changes, annual general meetings
- updating skills
  - for example standardizing training for a dispersed
    profession such as nursing
- back up with documentation, for example workbooks
  for open learning

Weaknesses
- relatively costly
- programmes must meet broadcast technical standards
- relies on target audience's motivation/ability to record
  programme
- an insecure medium, as it is broadcast to everyone with
  a television

Pitfalls
- could be seen as 'downmarket' television

Budget issues
- for non-urgent situations, more straightforward to send
  video-cassettes
- the savings made by not having to duplicate and
  distribute videos may not outweigh the costs of hiring
  transmitters

Timescales
- production issues as with video (see video, p. 76)
- requires advance booking

Activities
- set objectives
- negotiate and book slot on transmitters

- programme production process as for video (see video, p. 76), but to broadcast technical standards
- notify and motivate target audience

Feedback
- reply-paid cards

Measurement
- survey target audience to establish profile of those who recorded it, and those who ultimately watched the recording
- survey to measure retention of key messages

How to find out more
Using Television and Video in Business by Andrew Crofts, Mercury, 1991

International Visual Communications Association (IVCA), 2nd Floor, Bolsover House, 5/6 Clipstone St, London W1P 8LD 0171-580 0962

5 Computer-based communication

Letters, notes and memos
E-mail, bulletin boards and on-line conferences
Multimedia
Video with interaction
Documents on disk or via modem/network
The Internet
Intranets

LETTERS, NOTES AND MEMOS

Most formal business communication still appears on paper, but it's most often typed into a computer first – which is why letters, notes and memos appear in this chapter of the Guide rather than in Chapter 3. However, it's less the medium than the format, developed through many years of people doing business, that is of real interest to the communicator. Both offer a way of conveying information concisely and can subsequently act as an item of record for whatever purpose.

Of course, all three formats – and especially the memo – have been developed into art forms, not least by the 'Sir Humphreys' of this world, who are practised at using written communication to 'cover their backs' and to conceal rather than clarify their purpose, using a strange language known as memo-ese.

Once universally formal and very distinct from speech, the language now used in letters and especially today's instant memo format – the Post-it note – is becoming plainer and more open to the use of colloquial expression.

Strengths
- generally more private than many other methods
- can carry complex information
- gives you and the receiver a permanent record
- helps people focus on the action you want them to take
- allows/forces you to think through and revise what you want to say, putting emphasis on the right points
- can be very persuasive
- word-processed letters can be customized quickly for different people

Opportunities
- direct mail to people's homes, giving a much more 'personal' feel to the communication (with advantages and disadvantages)
- 'open-mail' systems, which enable people to send letters and memos through a central clearing house to senior managers; replies pass back through the clearing house which directs them to individuals, whose identity can be protected by a code system

Weaknesses	• takes time to plan and write
	• depending on people's personalities and educational backgrounds, written messages can be over-formal and bureaucratic, taking too long to read and too long to write; others can be too abrupt or poorly expressed, leading to misunderstanding
	• passes the action over to the receiver who may take a long time to reply
	• one-way communication
	• relies on efficient postal services; no record of sending or receipt on standard letters
	• insecure, depending on storage systems, in that they are easy for others to find and read, photocopy or even steal
Pitfalls	• tendency to become over-formal
	• mistakes undermine your credibility; proof-read your letter carefully
	• word-processing has introduced its own brand of errors; check carefully for nonsense which can pass through a spellcheck; check set letters that you 'cut and paste' together, you'll be so familiar with the content that you may miss pasting errors
Budget issues	• cost of generating and if necessary printing
	• cost of distribution when dealing with large mailing lists can often be a significant factor – but so can inclusion of letters in payslip packets for example
Timescales	• internal memos depend on the efficiency of the internal post
	• next day delivery
Activities	• set objectives
	• look at the standard of letter writing in your organization
	• consider establishing a house style, and creating model letters for common situations
	• consider offering training
Feedback	• survey people's preferred means of sending and receiving messages
	• survey people's views on the standard of written communication in the organization
Measurement	• compare the feedback responses over time

How to find out more   *Letters at Work* by A. Barker, Industrial Society Press, 1993
The only 250 Letters and Memos Managers will ever need by R. Tepper, John Wiley & Sons, 1994

E-MAIL, BULLETIN BOARDS AND ON-LINE CONFERENCES

The fact that average computers are becoming more powerful, and able to communicate with each other, has meant that many of the traditional communication media are simply transferring to computer. For example the humble memo or letter has achieved a new lease of life as electronic mail (e-mail). From your desk, you can send letters or even mailshots almost instantly to computers across the building or across the world, with equal ease – and what's more, monitor and analyse the response with ease.

Similarly, the notice-board now has an on-line equivalent – the 'bulletin board'. These can be established both as internal resources for project teams to track their progress and share ideas, and as external bulletin boards providing customers and suppliers with a forum to discuss issues without having to schedule time-consuming meetings. In a properly designed system, content can be updated by users as well as the central resource.

On-line conferences allow people to interact via the screen, for example, as opposed to travelling miles before propping up the bar at the real thing.

As information technology penetrates further into organizations, more and more people will acquire access to these services, marginalizing still further those without computers or knowledge of how to use them.

Strengths
- immediate, with a record of when created, when put on-line, and when accessed by the receiver
- can give people direct access to anyone, including senior management
- the ability to personalize general or routine messages
- once the facility is established, a cost-effective way of linking people worldwide
- avoids additional paper circulating the organization
- on-line meetings and conferences provide an opportunity for many people to give instant feedback, brainstorm and problem-solve
- bulletin boards and special interest forums provide a

defined area for fast information-giving and problem-solving
- e-mail messages can be receipted so the sender is immediately notified when the reader opens the message
- fast way of distributing text documents, such as newsletters, which can be printed locally or when needed
- all systems keep a record of sent e-mails so the problem of lost messages can be quickly traced
- attractive, particularly for younger groups
- a thriving subculture, with a relatively informal 'netiquette', with its own style and shorthand
  - for example IMO ('In My Opinion'), BTW ('By The Way'), WRT ('With Regard To'), FWIW (For What It's Worth), ROFL (Rolling on The Floor Laughing), BCNU (Be Seeing You)

Opportunities
- use computer 'kiosks' in public areas like the staff restaurant to give access to people without their own computer
- extend parts of the e-mail system to customers and suppliers, speeding all-round communication
- back up key communication with written support, such as a directory of all bulletin boards or fora
- support by archiving and indexing useful data

Weaknesses
- only reaches people with informed access to a computer, although others can rely on hard copy printed out nearby
- there is a temptation for users to send far too much, irrelevant, untargeted and unsolicited mail
  - training and awareness campaigns can help ensure that people target their mail
  - bulletin boards and fora can grow so fast that nobody has a clear idea what they contain
  - ideally someone needs to police and audit the system, identifying the material that should be archived from the dross that must be deleted
- no physical presence means that people can neglect to check their e-mail; software can provide automatic prompts, so that users see when their mail comes in
- e-mail is so fast that it can become a route for the grapevine (see grapevine, p. 139)
- needs to be downloaded to disk or laptop to be read at home or when travelling
- discipline needed to ensure that people do not waste

time 'surfing' the company's bulletin boards, fora and conferences

Pitfalls
- *'well, it's free, isn't it?'*
  - people see e-mail as 'free' communication, creating an undisciplined approach
- *'why do I need to talk to you?'*
  - its speed and ease can make people feel that they don't need to make face-to-face contact
- *'just dashed off an e-mail'*
  - e-mail is about as close as written contact gets to the speed of speech, and there is a tendency not to edit, revise or even read e-mail memos before they are sent
- public bulletin boards are prone to a phenomenon known as SPAMMING – tech-speak for the saturation of a newsgroup with inappropriate messages, usually of a commercial nature
  - if not confronted this can often render a group useless as the bulletin board fills up with advertisements
- many people still suffer from technofear when confronted by e-mail/bulletin board systems
- lack of understanding of 'netiquette' can cause problems (e.g. CAPITAL TEXT in e-mail terms is considered to be SHOUTING!)
- inappropriate/inefficient use of e-mail, for example jokes, chat, opinionated rants, etc.
- public systems are open to anyone with Internet access, including cyberstalkers, hackers and mailing list junkies

Budget issues
- many organizations will already use a Local Area Network (LAN) to link local communication, or a Wide Area Network (WAN) to link all sites, if not investment may be necessary for full networking
- alternatively, remote users, such as home workers, could log in via modem and phone line to 'pick up' their e-mail
- time spent using and administering the system

Timescales
- e-mail communication is virtually instant, but there is no guarantee when – or indeed *if* – the receiver will read it
- on-line conferencing ideally works in real time, ideas building on each other, or strands can be picked up

later, perhaps by people working on the other side of the world

Activities
- set objectives
- raise awareness and offer training in e-mail etiquette
- regulate the growth of e-mail
- oversee the running of conferences and bulletin boards

Feedback
- build feedback sessions into conferences
- within each forum or bulletin board, have a help section devoted to training and supporting users

Measurement
- it is vital to survey people to ensure that they are getting the information they want
- people accessing e-mail documents can be measured automatically
- compare effectiveness with other media
- measure how long it takes for readers to access their mail from the time it is created.

How to find out more
The Virtual Corporation by William H. Davidow and Michael F. Malone, Harper Business Press, 1993

MULTIMEDIA

Multimedia is still a buzzword open to broad interpretation and not fully understood by the general public. But it is also a sweeping, all-encompassing term, and as such reassuringly future-proofed.

At the moment it refers to computers combining text, video, sound, animated computer graphics, telecommunications, usually using a CD-ROM drive (compact disk read-only memory). There's yet to be a breakthrough application to make multimedia machines 'must haves' for everyone, but after early technical problems, hardware and software are settling down and the integration of all media into one is releasing tremendous synergy. For example it is revolutionizing computer-based training, by offering users very realistic simulations to participate in. We're all used to the help systems lying behind our software, but it is very reassuring to have a human face on screen calmly explaining what you have to do – the latest packages can feel like dealing with the Hal computer from *2001*.

If, as psychologists say, we retain about 20 per cent of what we hear, 30 per cent of what we see, and *50 per cent of what we hear and see*, the potential is there to create pieces of communication with real impact.

For example take a multimedia presentation about a particular organization – the modern equivalent of a corporate brochure. Circulated on CD-ROM or available on a network, this could be used as the 'bible' on how the organization works, with different levels of information for different purposes. The beauty is that, unlike video, it is non-linear – users determine what they see and in which order. It could be used, for example, as a general overview at induction, or to explain in detail the working of a particular process to an experienced project team. The networked version could be progressively updated, replacing old modules with new ones – minor changes would not mean discarding the entire programme, as it would with a corporate video.

Strengths
- combines strength of all media
  - print, video, CD-ROM, software
- totally flexible from users' point of view; they can

choose which options they want to see, and in what detail

- none of the users' time is wasted handling any material they do not need; they get instant access to what they want
- high impact presentations, using more of the audience's senses, aid retention of messages
- portability
  - multimedia presentations can be transferred electronically or on CD; end-users can run the software from the CD or download the files to their PC, allowing a single CD to supply an entire office
- presentations can be kept current via Internet updates and additional discs

Opportunities
- post conference support
  - see the speech being given, read it in synopsis or in full on screen, or print it out, view the slides, or any combination of these
- simulations for on-the-job training and education
  - for example using a sound card and a microphone to record a sequence into a dramatized situation, such as recording a response to an angry bank customer
  - lets the trainee practise interactions without the need for time-consuming 'real-time' role-plays
  - possible to keep a record of a person's progress through a module
- use multimedia 'kiosks' in public areas like the staff restaurant to give access to people without their own multimedia computer
- use for interactive marketing
  - for example displays in foyers, exhibitions, hands-on museum exhibits
  - person using it gets fully involved with your 'advert'
- back up multimedia with written support, preferably giving the audience a route map showing how to find your way around a multimedia package

Weaknesses
- multimedia software is not very user-friendly, and not always very compatible with specific hardware
- multimedia authoring is something of a new skill, and many people are learning 'on the job'
- multimedia can put a great demand on the memory of machines; even when the memory is boosted to compensate, power-hungry material like video sequences can slow down performance

- a multimedia project represents a huge investment of time and specialist skill: considerable timescales are involved in the development of multimedia systems – interface design, programming, art and testing are critical elements to be considered
- we know how to produce the individual media within multimedia, but we're still learning how to put all those parts together to best effect
  - it's rather like knowing the words of a language without knowing the grammar
  - there are few successful models to guide people on how to structure multimedia 'documents'
  - thinking in a non-linear way is demanding, you no longer have the security of a 'beginning', 'middle' and 'end', because to a large degree the 'structure' is defined by the audience
- the design of interfaces and functionality must be carefully considered to avoid users becoming confused or bored by the system

Pitfalls
- still-developing technology
  - designers enjoy the challenge of using the latest multimedia software, and will push it to the limit, with the danger that the objectives of the programme, and its budget and schedule, will be lost in the name of 'art', which, more truthfully, is experimentation
- similarly, there's a tendency to produce flashy, over-engineered software which forgets the message and tends to be light on content
- audiences must be targeted quite specifically
  - in terms of corporate culture, technical ability and system capability (*'sorry, our machines can't read it'*)
- burying options
  - some 'documents' lose flexibility by building in long, linear sequences, effectively hiding the material from the users, or forcing them down a particular path to get to the information they want
- upgrade-mania
  - multimedia authoring software is ever-improving, but it is not always easy to upgrade existing presentations into the new software, which shortens its effective shelf life
- *'whose profession is this anyway?'*
  - by definition, multimedia works across all disciplines
  - ideally you need a project team strong in all the

media represented, run by someone with a clear
unifying vision
- without a strong, shared vision, multimedia teams
  can pull in opposite directions, or worse, omit one
  of the disciplines, for example the software experts
  writing text or directing videos, or writers believing
  they can create graphics
- consider security issues carefully, bearing in mind the
  portability of the media involved

Budget issues
- supplementing existing hardware
  - upgrading current hardware vs buying new
    multimedia hardware packages
- authoring software
- buying in or subcontracting the main project skill areas
  involved in multimedia authoring

Timescales
- equipment and off-the-shelf software can be bought
  and running almost immediately
- at least three months' intensive effort from a
  multidisciplined project team to create a professional-
  looking multimedia program

Activities
- set objective
- write plan and approve
- storyboard
- test the storyboard on a target sample audience
- 'build' a crude prototype
- test the prototype on a target sample
- source and create material
  - video, audio, computer animation, graphics and text
- build a prototype combining all elements
- test the new prototype on a target sample
- revise and de-bug
- when approved, press on to CD-ROM and distribute,
  or place on a network

Feedback
- invite feedback on screen, for example as a prompt
  when the user exits a multimedia program

Measurement
- retention of key messages
- study to check usability and to see which options are
  most popular

How to find out more
International Visual Communications Association (IVCA),
2nd Floor, Bolsover House, 5/6 Clipstone St, London
W1P 8LD 0171-580 0962

VIDEO WITH INTERACTION

The danger with standard video is that it is becoming so familiar and seductive that it can leave the audience unchallenged, just passively absorbed in letting the material wash over them with the same degree of attention they pay a TV soap, (or indeed, not even that much).

The philosophy of interactive video is to challenge the viewers, asking them to make certain choices or posing questions before they proceed. This has entered a new era through computer-based multimedia (see multimedia, p. 98) but there is still a role for using ordinary video-recorders, structured for interaction.

Strengths
- relatively low-tech, accessible to anyone with a video-recorder
- helps to illustrate, structure and punctuate events
- good for conveying target behaviours, improving performance
  - can show the outcomes of different courses of action
  - makes abstract choices concrete by showing these consequences – demonstrating 'what-if' scenarios

Opportunities
- boost involvement through questions, choices and exercises
- use interactive video for specific purposes
  - for example recruitment, induction, training
- by using two or more videos you can simulate the effect of choosing different routes, as with computer-based interactive video
- for full interaction treat it like an open learning package with worksheets and follow-up exercises

Weaknesses
- because video is a linear medium, it cannot match the level of interactivity available via multimedia (see multimedia, p. 98)
- the structure is fairly rigid; it assumes you want to go through all the exercises and questions with each audience
- difficult to access specific parts of the tape

Pitfalls
- 'the blindingly obvious choice'
  - some interactive videos can be rather patronizing,

with very obvious choices, resembling old-style government public information films
- 'Hobson's choice'
  - because the element of choice offered is frequently very limited, the user's true course of action may not be represented

Budget issues
- cost of designing and producing interactive video programme, and its supporting documentation
- cost of viewing facilities

Timescales
- minimum of three months for a good quality product, tailored to need

Activities
- set objectives
- pull together team to design, test and produce programme
- duplicate, use and monitor
- arrange viewing facilities

Feedback
- questionnaires after use

Measurement
- compare with objectives
  - for example improvement in target behaviours by comparing with measurements taken before the programme is used

How to find out more
International Visual Communications Association (IVCA), 2nd Floor, Bolsover House, 5/6 Clipstone St, London W1P 8LD 0171-580 0962

DOCUMENTS ON DISK OR VIA MODEM/NETWORK

The amount of time and effort wasted by people still re-inputting text, or even recreating content from scratch, is truly alarming. Through a simple operation, that text can now be shared on disk, or sent via modem or over a network, anywhere in the world.

We have yet to see a quantum leap in sharing data in this way, despite the increased compatibility of systems. To some extent the problem is attitudinal rather than technological. People are reluctant to share information that they've worked hard to get, or which gives them some power, or takes effort – even the smallest – to share.

But sharing data for the good of the organization is in theory for the good of the individuals involved, as they'll benefit in turn from the work of others. The more evidence of success is publicized, the earlier people will begin to make the effort required.

Perhaps that will be the point where people become more disciplined about file nomenclature. At present, unfortunately, most information sits in eccentrically named files, buried seemingly at random in an individual's subdirectories, doing the electronic equivalent of gathering dust. How many of us can say that if we disappeared under that proverbial bus, anyone else in our organization could find their way around our filing systems?

This communication blockage will only be removed if business as a whole can resolve the ethical and intellectual property issues – in short decide who has *practical* ownership of a document.

If someone generates a document in the organization's time, using its resources, then surely that organization has a right to expect that person to store that document in such a way that the whole organization can benefit from it? The technology exists, the potential benefits are great, but the intellectual and psychological challenge is enormous.

Strengths
- high portability of information
  - instant delivery via network or modem
  - high capacity on disk, easily posted across the world
- rapid sharing of knowledge, spreading of best practice
- documents can be customized, and used for different purposes by different receivers

Opportunities
- introduce document control systems
  - for example showing who created a document, when and where it was generated, the draft number, the software it was written in
  - it is hard enough to keep track of different drafts of the same document, but even harder with multiple sites producing their own version of documents
- create a file index
  - to prevent organizations constantly reinventing the wheel a central index describing key files on the network would provide the best starting point for any project
- standardize file naming and file describing protocols
  - people could search the organization's database for self-explanatory filenames, or by keywords
- introduce a 'clippings' service
  - use software to enable people to set their systems to 'browse' the organization's databases on a regular basis, identifying all documents containing keywords of their choice
  - useful for skills updating or for monitoring developments in a particular field
- how fast you can retrieve and manage key information is a vital source of competitive advantage, and if you are getting this right, it makes sense to push this message to your outside customers through marketing or PR

Weaknesses
- lack of central control
  - individuals edit and rewrite documents as they want
- lack of control over own files
  - it may be hard to convince people that anyone else should have access to their work
  - they may overcompensate by password-protecting too many of their files
- not much good for technophobes
  - it could marginalize anyone lacking the necessary computer or research skills

- distributing electronically relies on the receiver to take action to access and use the file
  - as opposed to passively receiving a document
- people like paper – it's familiar, physical, they can write on it, and it's easy to file
  - in most cases there will be a hard copy duplicate of documents
- exposure to the Data Protection Act
  - in theory, certain sensitive data should not be computerized in any way
- increased risk of virus damage
  - computer security protocols are becoming increasingly important as information is shared from system to system, over disk or networks

Pitfalls
- not the paperless office
  - systems still crash and disks corrupt from time to time
- untrained people
  - outside the computer industry, the standard of computer training tends to be low, with many users just expected to learn as they go
- overloaded networks
  - organizations often push overloaded networked systems past their limits, with too many users making demands at peak times, slowing tasks down

Budget issues
- cost-benefit analysis of local vs central document production
- investment in dedicated communication lines (Local Area Networks or Wide Area Networks)
- alternatively investment in software to link PCs on-line via modem when needed
- training and resource

Timescales
- most organizations can now transfer files on disk between systems
- to transfer data on-line from one system to another involves the time taken to buy, fit, and learn to use a modem

Activities
- research and set up appropriate etiquette and work systems
- set objectives
- run an awareness campaign to highlight the cost of re-inputting text and citing cases of unnecessary re-work
- organize a training campaign, if needed
- set up a central information resource

- introduce networking systems if appropriate

Feedback
- most software will verify and confirm that a file has been successfully transferred – posting a disk relies on a call to check that it has arrived and works
- if you are using someone else's files, it is usually courtesy and good practice to let them know what you're doing – they may also be able to offer further help

Measurement
- cost-benefit analysis for different methods of transferring data
  - for example rather than printing and sending a paper document around the world, you could simply send the text electronically, and print out locally
- record of files being used and transferred

How to find out more
- identify bulk senders and receivers of text within and outside the organization, talk through their needs with them
- invite lots of suppliers in (competition is tough so they'll happily do it for free) for advice and awareness sessions
- identify parallel organizations that are sharing data effectively and visit them to see how they do it

The Virtual Corporation by William H. Davidow and Michael F. Malone, Harper Business Press, 1993

THE INTERNET

The Internet is a global network of over twenty million users, ranging from government offices to corporations, from individuals and universities to businesses of all kinds.

At the time of writing, there are still difficulties in proving its practical worth as a business tool, but the potential is too exciting to ignore. Even now, the network is so huge that finding your way around it can seem impossible, rather like seeing the big toe of an elephant, and trying to imagine the whole beast from it.

To make it more of a challenge the Internet thrives like a grapevine, and has an organic, totally flexible 'structure'. It makes mapping it out difficult, and means that most of the literature in the field dates very quickly.

What it does do is bring the world to your desk over a local gateway. That is, for the cost of a local call, you can use the modem on your computer to tap into a node on the global network through a service provider. It will handle the connection, and give guidance on where to find particular information. Alternatively, with the right hardware and software, you can access the Internet directly yourself by making an agreement with a site you are interested in, and dialling its number.

In a business context, once connected to the network you can use it to search newspaper or magazine databases for all the articles written on a particular subject, scan business reports, check the financial health of a company, keep up to date with share options, and in the same way find the best rail route from Dresden to Darlington.

The Internet unites people of like interests and expertise, pooling the world's information resources. Increasingly intelligent and sophisticated search programs are helping to manage the information, making the systems capable of filtering out just the data you are looking for.

Rather like real surfing, surfing the Internet is a highly skilled process – sometimes you hit the crest of a wave and find the very information you're looking for, but at other times you may be paddling through more than a little software 'sewage'.

Strengths
- ever-growing
- access to outside databases/contributors worldwide
- e-mail gateway for customers and suppliers
- strong appeal to the computer-literate within your internal audience

Opportunities
- closer contact with customers, suppliers and peers
  - for example on-line conferences, bulletin boards, help forums (see e-mail, bulletin boards, etc., p. 94)
- can provide an instant on-line research resource

Weaknesses
- software to access it is still rather unfriendly
- requires fairly high skill levels
- needs software protection protocols to be strictly followed
- security issues
  - danger of sensitive files being accessed from the network
  - danger of virus being introduced into the organization
- real cost ignored
  - people tend to think of the cost of a local call, but pricing structures can be more complicated
  - for example expect high charges for access to premium databases

Pitfalls
- finding yourself chasing novelty value
  - to some extent the Internet is still an incredible solution looking for an application
- opening up a browser's paradise
  - part of the Internet's emotional attraction is the fact that so little of it has been explored
  - browsing and exploring is somewhat addictive, and can be expensive both in time and in extra usage charges
- sex, lies and videogames
  - unlike service providers such as CompuServe, an on-line information service that helps structure access to the Internet, the Internet itself is not under anyone's specific control; organizations have encountered the problem of people accessing very dubious or sensitive material, spreading commercial rumours and, most commonly, simply downloading and playing the latest computer games
  - any organization with a computer needs a clearly

defined computer security policy, and this needs to be strengthened and enforced when you are able to access outside networks
- put disciplinary guidelines in place to discourage people from abusing the system – it may not prevent them from inadvertently downloading a virus, but it will at least stop them from using 'pin up' windows, and playing games in work time

Budget issues
- most organizations will already have the necessary and simple hardware – a modem and computer
- investment in software to improve access to the Internet, and ability to search for data
- subscription to a gateway service
  - for example membership of CompuServe or Delphi to give you local access to the network
- time spent in learning how to use the software, and identifying useful contacts and databases around the Internet

Timescales
- given that you can access it with fairly basic hardware, most organizations already have potential access to the Internet
- signing up with a gateway service provider will take around two weeks

Activities
- set objectives
- research hardware and software requirements
  - talk to your IT department
  - read computer magazines for contact addresses
- take out subscription to a gateway provider if appropriate
- go on-line to carry out tasks, for example global on-line research or e-mailing outside your own organization

Feedback
- instant feedback on-line or via e-mail

Measurement
- measure usage and popular destinations
- cost-benefit analysis of different research methods, for example in-house vs out-of-house, library vs on-line services

How to find out more
The Internet Guide for New Users by Daniel P. Dern, McGraw-Hill, 1994
The Virtual Corporation by William H. Davidow and Michael F. Malone, Harper Business Press, 1993

CompuServe, PO Box 676, Bristol BS99 IYN 0117 927 8000

UKONLINE, The Maltings, Charlton Road, Shepton
Mallet, Somerset, BA4 5QE 0645 000011
HyperCAST, Duke Street House, 50 Duke Street, London
W1M 5DS 0171-290 9500

INTRANETS

Perhaps the most revolutionary of all the IT advances affecting IC are intranets, which have enormous potential to benefit the organization. The biggest dilemma for those involved in start-ups is the extent to which to give maximum spur to creativity and involvement by allowing the intranet to grow naturally – imposing no etiquette or style guides – and accepting the potential for chaos, which may not be that easy to recover from.

Strengths
- people are more inclined to make use of information presented in this way because they themselves 'pull down' what they want, rather than being forced to accept what's 'pushed' at them
- stimulates people to take more responsibility for seeking and finding information, also prompts them naturally to get involved in ideas and networking, thereby promoting a more interactive and 'empowered' culture
- allows the development of a shared internal resource, online administration and communication within a company
- one step closer to the paperless office – removal of administration and filing
- news and current developments may be communicated quickly via e-mail and news services
- public areas may be set up to link into the world wide web
- public terminals may be set up in reception areas to communicate more about the company – thereby avoiding the cost of a standalone multimedia product, for example
- obvious repository (and nursery) for the organization's intellectual capital

Opportunities
- increased innovation
  - big stimulus for having and sharing ideas
- increased security
  - only those users with the correct authority can have access and all may be monitored for misuse of the system
- increased efficiency and speed
  - huge savings on learning curves as people share information on how to do this or that

– significant time and cost savings are available by substituting for print products or call centres, for example

Weaknesses
- impersonal
  - users have less interaction with others and may find the system somewhat cold, especially if it's not user-friendly
  - on the other hand, the impersonal aspect is why some people like it (engineers seem to be favourites for this, but also more generally, anyone who is more confident in writing than speaking mode when communicating at work)
- like any medium, it attracts the verbose and the self-promoting (who may spend more time on it than they should), but perhaps it's a better way of letting off steam than face to face and at least the rest of us have a choice whether or not to 'listen'
- the IT department may think it should be designing/controlling the intranet, rather than helping out with the technical side, which can lead to problems of internal politics

Pitfalls
- interface and functionality must match both the technical knowledge of the users and the style and culture of the company, otherwise you will be wasting time and effort

Budget issues
- setting up the basic sites and materials can take considerable resource, not just from a dedicated individual or team but from others in the organization with whom they must liaise to get the design and initial content right
- if you want everyone to use it, everyone must have access to a PC and a modem, receive training and be allowed time to use it
- the cost of providing off-site access (i.e. via a modem) is not insignificant – it's worth assessing the need and building such considerations into the design

Timescales
- between six and eight months to go live, depending on the size of your organization and the extent of your initial ambitions
- it's not actually that difficult to set up the systems – the time is spent bringing the right people together and securing the right buy-in at all levels

Activities	• assemble a steering team of enlightened and keen people – make sure key departments are represented
	• set initial objectives, cost parameters and timetables
	• research hardware and software requirements
	  – talk to your IT department
	  – research what people might want/have to gain from an intranet
	  – discover what's available in the way of potential materials to kickstart a library
	• talk to potential suppliers of software and implementation consultancy
	• prepare a business case and obtain appropriate resources/budget
	• design and run a pilot
	• develop a training and installation programme
	• create an ongoing support and maintenance regime

Feedback	• relay usage results (in factual and anecdotal terms) to encourage active participation
Measurement	• measure usage and popular destinations • cost-benefit analysis of different research methods, for example in-house vs out-of-house, library vs on-line services
How to find out more	• most communication consultancies offer some kind of advice service: choose one with a demonstrable track record in setting up a system (including running internal workshops etc.) and which has the resource to go beyond 'modelling' and give you any technical advice/practical help you need • we can't recommend a specific book but conferences on the subject abound • if you don't attend a conference, make direct contact with speakers who claim to have 'been there, done it' – try to gain some live, hands-on experience of finding your way around on their intranet

6 Organizational communication

Corporate identity
Symbolic communication
Participative structures
Working environment
Public display
Award schemes
Focus groups, surveys and research
Grapevine
Networking
Public relations, news management and
marketing
Advertising

CORPORATE IDENTITY

Everything an organization does says something about its values and personality (see the sections on symbolic communication and working environment pp. 122 and 129). This is nowhere more apparent than in the visible components of an organization's corporate identity – in its crudest form its corporate colours, logo, headed notepaper, lorries, uniforms and so on.

Consciously revising your organization's corporate identity is often a classic, if extremely valuable case of 'the tail wagging the dog'.

It's only when we sit down to decide what we want to 'say' about ourselves that we start examining the fundamental and painful questions about our organization:

- *who* are we?
- *why* are we here?
- *what* are we trying to do?
- *how* do we do what we do?

According to the UK corporate identity industry's godfather, Wally Olins, it is the 'yardstick' against which an organization's products, behaviours and actions are measured.

Typically, people think about corporate identity as the *physical* things that can be updated, the signs, uniforms and so on, but its advocates believe it does much more. It can provide a clear symbol that things have changed. It can also redirect and re-energize employees and reinforce the commitment of other stakeholder audiences.

Corporate identity is a booming field, with the public sector heavily involved, from healthcare trusts to individual schools, from the 'new' universities to government agencies. The successful players are highly specialized. Developing corporate identity is a combination of management consultancy and design expertise. To the extent that it's usually not wise to cut your own hair, it may be a mistake to handle a corporate identity revamp in-house – you're just too close to the problem.

Strengths
- re-energizing
- communicating change
- motivating
- restating the organization's values

Opportunities
- involve internal audiences in research and testing
- involve them in the communication campaign
  - for example a party on the day of the launch
- as a public relations exercise, donate obsolete stationery to charities of employees' choice
- involve employees in auditing everything that needs to be updated
  - the list may be daunting, and this will be an opportunity to decide if all the variations of memos, forms, letterheads, compliment slips and so on are *really* needed, thus avoiding criticisms that too much is being spent on the change

Weaknesses
- the cost, with leading players charging at least a million for a corporate identity programme
- the change will be cosmetic if not a true reflection of the organization and its values
- this may mean it has to follow or be accompanied by a programme to change attitudes and behaviours
- can be seen as a waste of money or a luxury option in times of cost control
- a soft target for people to attack, very hard to quantify in terms of benefits
- requires superb project management and logistics skill
- you can't please all the people all the time
  - if you were successful with your last corporate ID, people will take time to be persuaded to your new one

Pitfalls
- inadequate research
  - in hurrying the research phase, you miss the important opportunity for involvement and testing designs, resorting instead to arbitrarily imposing a solution
- patchy update
  - inevitably, corporate identity has to be phased in over a period, but nothing looks more unprofessional than a mix of identities; wherever possible, make sure no one can use an old identity by mistake
- doing it yourself/using a cheap supplier

- an amateurish or second-class identity represents an amateurish or second-class organization
- local empires
  - departments and sites may try to make unauthorized adaptations of the corporate standards
  - diluting the 'brand' by introducing too many variants
- unclear or hidden corporate standards
  - in many cases, internal audiences are ignorant of the fact that there *are* standards controlling how logos are used, documents laid out and so on; put a clearly written corporate standards file in every department, explaining in plain English how the identity should appear, and include a contact number for colour copies of logos, bromides, etc.; for immediacy, circulate the standards on disk or network them
- too often
  - 'fiddling' with the identity, or relaunching the whole identity too often, literally does create 'identity crises', moving the cultural goal posts and leaving internal and external audiences confused about what the organization actually stands for
- lack of vision
  - there is a danger of conservatism, merely 'tweaking' the existing identity because of organizational inertia
  - the objectives may be too vague or abstract, for example 'we want to be a "world class" organization'
  - blandness – 'me too' identities based on other design models rather than organizational values
- fashion
  - some corporate identities become classics, others date because they are too closely tied to what is in vogue in graphic design at the time
- short shelf life
  - it's easy to forget to plan ahead for contingencies, for example how many companies wasted paper on 'phone day', by not predicting stationery usage?
- ugly, uncomfortable uniforms
  - walk down any high street, and even today you will find some spectacularly demeaning uniforms, some even designed to match the carpets
  - question the need for uniforms in the first place
  - people are only going to feel confident and motivated

if they've been involved in choosing the design of
the uniform, and it's very clearly been tested

Budget issues
- time spent defining objectives, working up proposed identities and testing them
- time spent in planning and implementing the identity
- materials bill including new signage, livery, packaging, products, publications, vehicles, advertising/ marketing materials
- cost of awareness campaign
- if you have in-house capability, it's a question of how far you involve outside consultants
  - for example they may help with the initial design concepts and research and you handle the practical implementation

Timescales
- for large organizations, introducing a new corporate identity will take a minimum of six months

Activities
- set objectives for the new identity
- define, commission and test designs by seeing how they are perceived by target groups
- run an awareness campaign as a 'teaser' for the new launch
- draw up an implementation plan
- put the plan into action
  - explain to people what the identity means for them
  - update the physical materials – logos, livery, uniform, stationery, T-shirts and so on
- audit the identity
  - ensure that all evidence of previous identities has been removed, including 'personal' stocks of old letterhead, forms, etc. which may creep back into the system
- research periodically to make sure identity has not dated

Feedback
- invite employees, customers, suppliers, shareholders for their input into the design
- survey all target groups as you develop the identity

Measurement
- comparing reaction of target groups against identity

How to find out more
The Corporate Image: strategies for effective identity programmes by Nicholas Ind, Kogan Page, 1990
Corporate Reputation: managing the new strategic asset by John Smythe, Colette Dorward and Jerome Reback, Century Business, 1992

The New Guide to Identity by Wolff Olins, Gower/The Design Council, 1996

SYMBOLIC COMMUNICATION

Consistent messages are vital in communication. The challenge in internal communication is that what we say is often not what we do. Action speaks louder than words, especially in the context of employee communication, where the audience can be suspicious of organizational propaganda. Bold promises, cynically made, are received on the ground even more cynically.

Symbolic communication is not so much a medium to control, more as they say, 'a way of life'. It covers everything from the organization's values, the management style, the way employees are treated through to the corporate body's social responsibilities. As such it's the territory of everyone from general management consultants to organizational psychologists, from ergonomists, even to anthropologists.

Employees (and suppliers) are whole people, so if they're demotivated and not performing, the diagnosis has to be a holistic one. There will be a wide range of reasons why people are unhappy, and why the star performers you are after wouldn't touch your organization with a bargepole. Regular and detailed attitude surveys will start to give you clues why.

This section will look in more detail at some of the factors lying behind the organizational façade and give examples of some of the practical steps you can take. Actions do speak loudest of all, but they are also the hardest medium to control.

Organization values What messages do you send people about the values of your organization? For example via:

- job titles
- visible status symbols
  - for example type of office, thickness of carpet, size of window
- how redundancy is handled
  - coldly handed a bin bag and escorted from the premises
  - with sensitivity, investing in outplacement
- uniforms

– the style denotes the public image the company has of itself (which may not match the audience's notion)

Management style What messages do you send to people through the way managers are allowed or encouraged to behave? For example:

- commanding or empowering
- means of address
  – for example on first name terms with all
- tacit acceptance of aggression, bullying and victimization
- socializing with the team, or keeping their distance
- tolerating humour or welcoming it
- leading by example
  – a leading Japanese businessman recently said, 'I would be ashamed to take a pay rise higher than my team'
  – 'mucking in when crisis hits'

Buildings and facilities What message do people pick up from your buildings? For example:

- choice of office
  – a high-tech unit on a business park
  – an imposing tower block
  – a friendly Georgian house
- the state of the building
  – how secure can people feel if the organization appears not to invest in maintaining the building?
- number of people per square foot
- overloaded infrastructure
  – poor ventilation, inadequate heating, little natural daylight, lack of meeting places, poor telecommunication, computing, toilet and kitchen facilities
- can employees be *effective* within it?
  – if you're not 'empowered' even to open a window, you hardly feel valued in your job
- catering facilities
  – the acid test of single status restaurants is not the layout, nor the principle that management and workers can eat together, but whether they actually *do*
- extra facilities like open learning centres, workplace nurseries and access to sports facilities

Employee respect   How do employees (and suppliers) feel they are treated?
For example:

- balancing needs
  - are they respected as whole people who need to look
    after family as well as work interests?
- personal and career development
  - does the organization play an active role in
    supporting it?
- decision-making
  - are your people involved, especially in decisions
    directly affecting them?
- listening
  - do people feel that they can really make a difference?
- dress code
  - is it demeaning, or can it be deliberately subverted,
    for example 'dress down' days when employees
    can dress casually?

Social responsibility   Where does the organization stand in terms of business
ethics, supporting charities, and working with the local
community? For example:

- supporting the local community
- running office/works tours
- family days
- encouraging voluntary work, secondments to local
  charities
- building links with schools and colleges
- producing educational packs

Strengths
- symbolic communication is at the heart of the
  organization
  - positive impact here will communicate to employees
    and beyond
- symbolic communication is active – the organization is
  'putting its money where its mouth is'

Opportunities
- any new management style has to be demonstrated
  from the top by senior management
  - reinforce this with an awareness campaign
  - introduce upward appraisal
- if you have a depressing, inefficient building, consider
  handing the problem over to the people who work
  in it – they know best what they need to perform
  effectively
- take every opportunity to consult people on issues that
  affect them

– people will only buy in to decisions if they have been explained to them
– imposing decisions is counterproductive in the long run because people can find a million ways to undermine situations that they do not agree with

Weaknesses
- symbolic communication is essentially a symptom rather than a cause – you can be aware of it, but ultimately you need to tackle the fundamental problems that are holding back your people
- massive investment in a communication and change programme may be necessary to have a big impact on how an organization behaves

Pitfalls

Alienation
- by challenging the status quo, you may unsettle those who are comfortable with it
  – for example introducing empowerment to a culture where managers traditionally have control will make managers feel insecure

Human engineering
- organizations are like delicate ecosystems – changing any element in the environment, whether it's the way employees are treated, the building, the management style or its social responsibility policies, will have an effect on the rest
  – some people may like the change, others will not

Budget issues
- funding attitude research

Timescales
- the quest to manage attitudes with greater awareness through symbolic communication is ongoing

Activities
- set objectives
- attitude change campaigns and training workshops

Feedback
- use all media to gather feedback

Measurement
- it is difficult to define the items that make up symbolic communication, but it is easy to measure the impact it has through attitude and opinion surveys
- also measure changing factors in the organization through regular exit interviews

How to find out more
The Power of Empowerment by David Clutterbuck and Sue Kernaghan, Kogan Page, 1994
The New Guide to Identity by Wolff Olins, Gower/The Design Council, 1996

PARTICIPATIVE STRUCTURES

Whatever your political stance on unions, they were a direct channel of communication to employees and an identified structure for employee representation. Best practice suggests that employees *do* need a way to be more involved in the running of organizations. How far can empowerment go, if employees' scope for decision-making is so limited?

Rather than being feared, face-to-face communication between management and some sort of employee representative group can help explain the background to difficult decisions, even if organizations are not going to go beyond such legal obligations as exist to consult employees on certain issues.

Some companies favour shared ownership as a means of stimulating participation, sometimes offering employees shares at a discount rate, but while this is financial participation, there's not much opportunity to have a say in the business outside the AGM.

Other organizations favour joint consultative committees, working in partnership to tackle business issues. Then there is the plethora of *ad hoc* teams, such as service or quality improvement teams, concerned with particular tasks. The tide is currently flowing in favour of more formal employee representation, such as works councils, although there are signs that continental Europe (from whence the idea emanated) is beginning to re-think the cost implications for businesses.

Strengths
- creates a climate where ideas and commitment are valued
- route for upward feedback from target audiences
- channel for management to deal directly with the people concerned
- demonstrates a clear commitment to consultation

Opportunities
- jointly produced documents or jointly run projects that are in the mutual interest of the organization and the target group
  - for example producing guides on personal safety

- involving group representatives in aspects of the communication process
  - they may be more trusted
  - they can help keep internal media on track with the issues employees care about
  - for example employees could be members of editorial committees

Weaknesses
- management fear lack of control and misinterpretation of messages
- time-consuming
- everything relies on the assumption that the people on the committees are truly representative of employees
- can create expectations of involvement in decision-making which managers are not prepared to cede

Pitfalls
- once a consultation process is established, it may be perceived as a right and be very hard to take away or ignore
- the process needs to be managed carefully to avoid creating a bodged, compromised outcome, all too obviously the product of a committee of diverse views
- singing one's own praises on consultation, either within or outside the organization, before you're sure the target group would agree with you

Budget issues
- time spent preparing and meeting

Timescales
- if consultation is not in place it may take many months to set up a successful process

Activities
- set objectives
- research best practice in employee consultation to choose a model appropriate for the culture
  or
- run meetings within existing infrastructure

Feedback
- regular meetings act as a forum for feedback
- employee attitudes surveys

Measurement
- impact of employee consultation on the organization

How to find out more
Employee Communications and Consultation, ACAS Publications, 1994

Your Employees – Your Edge in the 1990s, Smythe, Dorward, Lambert, 1990

New Developments in Employee Involvement by Mick Marchington, John Goodman and Adrian Wilkinson, Employment Department, 1992

'Employee communication and participation' by Chris

Brewster and Ariane Hegewisch, *P+European Participation Monitor*, Number 7, 1993

'Writing wrongs with democracy' by Anat Arkin, *Personnel Management Plus*, April 1994 (Study of John Lewis' consultative and communication mechanisms)

'Employee involvement: employees' views' by Christine Tillsley, *Employment Gazette*, June 1994

Empowering People at Work by Nancy Foy, Gower, 1994

Involvement and Participation Association, 42 Colebrooke Row, London N1 8AF 0171-354 8040

ACAS Public Enquiries, 83/117 Euston Road, London NW1 2RB 0171-396 5100

WORKING ENVIRONMENT

Most organizations want their employees to contribute more ideas and be more creative. For example they go to great lengths to run award schemes that reward ideas and innovation (see award schemes, p. 134) and service improvement teams, yet it may be the organization itself that is stifling creativity.

From outside, many organizations look like they were deliberately designed to stamp out any creative thought, from rigid rulebooks to dingy conditions, from the soulless office to performance management systems that put the emphasis on the *management* rather than the *performance* (see symbolic communication, p. 122).

It's no surprise that some of the best breakthroughs happen through conversations. One thought will spark off another. The art is somehow to capture the benefits of the sort of creative interplay that goes on around coffee machines across the world, as well as what emerges in more formal meetings.

Strongly creative people by definition find a way around the rigidities of the bureaucratic organization. They break all the rules, rub the boss up the wrong way, and make themselves generally hell to manage.

But what about most employees? What can be done to release their creativity?

Strengths

Workplace
- immediately visible as a sign of commitment to the well-being and productivity of individuals
- affects *everyone*, not just those who typically read or listen
- no special expenditure needed – just thought
- stimulates appropriate behaviours unconsciously

Working methods
- improvements in working methods reflect and support other positive activities like quality and customer care

Opportunities
- involve individuals in improving their work area
  - ideally ask them to plan what they would do within a set budget
  - each area or team will establish its own identity and set up creative corners

Weaknesses
- it's hard to define creative behaviours
  - by definition creativity does not lend itself to reductive competency statements
- creative tensions are a necessary part of any creative process, but can be counterproductive if managers are unskilled

Pitfalls

Workplace layouts
- replacing one rigid structure with another
  - organizational needs and teams change constantly, so any new layout needs to be just as adaptable
- *'but this is what you asked for'*
  - as with any consultation exercise, make sure that you've consulted everyone who will be affected, not just those who shout loudest

Working systems
- *'what's really valued here?'*
  - competency statements are notorious for being vague and unclear
  - define clear performance standards
  - be wary of off-the-peg competency statements, test them first on your employees
- *'if I'm not paid extra for it, why do it?'*
  - you can't itemize every behaviour
- *'my boss'll never give me credit'*
  - if the performance standards are clear, there should be less variation in how managers rate employees
  - build in an arbitration process, and make the performance management system more objective by 'cross-marking'
- *'my boss only listens to them'*
  - be wary of favouring employees perceived as 'creative'; you may be setting up élitism, and holding back other employees

Budget issues
- cost of creating new, flexible layouts; in fact, hot-desking and utilizing restaurants as meeting areas are cost-saving exercises

Timescales
- ties in with existing initiatives

Activities
- set objectives
- research to identify what employees feel would help them be more creative and make more of a contribution to the organization
- look for a more flexible approach to office design, mixing employees, breaking down 'little empires'

- for example organizations are introducing central areas where employees can 'hot-desk', simply dropping in to use a work station or meet with colleagues
- one of the benefits of hot-desking is that people from different functions automatically network with each other because there are no fixed territories
- set up working areas in the restaurant or 'public' areas like an atrium, utilizing space that is not fully utilized through most of the day and can be a pleasant, informal working or meeting place
- clarify objectives, goals and standards and then empower employees to meet them however they want to
- if people feel they can add value, and have more scope to operate, they are more likely to take risks
- pool talents, for example cross-functionally, as new perspectives 'bouncing off each other' may create fresh ideas
- where appropriate, encourage employees to work from customers' sites, improving their understanding of customer's needs, which they can communicate back to the organization

Feedback
- employee involvement in designing a more creative environment

Measurement
- productivity measurements
- analysis of successful creative ideas
- monitor use of communal areas

How to find out more
The New Guide to Identity by Wolff Olins, Gower/The Design Council, 1996

The Virtual Corporation by William H. Davidow and Michael F. Malone, Harper Business Press, 1993

PUBLIC DISPLAY

Notice-boards carry everything from the menu in the staff restaurant to flat shares, car sales and quality submissions. A quirky hybrid of bureaucratese and street talk, part of their charm is that they are 'public', open to everyone.

Posters are a clear way of getting a simple message across, especially in industrial environments.

Strengths
- notice-boards give sense of community, familiarity and joint ownership
- posters leave a constant reminder
- equal access to everyone

Opportunities
- involve employees in taking ownership of the notice-boards, clearing off old messages when they become dated
- dedicate part of a board to anonymous feedback on specific issues, letting off steam
- posters can be made interactive, for example requiring people to fill in key organizational measurements in terms of sales, clients served and so on

Weaknesses
- notice-boards and posters are a fairly passive medium, relying on people to read them as they pass by
- remember notice-boards are a public medium, so all visitors will see them

Pitfalls

Notice-boards
- not updated or managed
  - become messy and chaotic, carrying curling sheets
- not formatted
  - just an information dump
- inconsistent design
  - difficult to find the information you need
- not read at a glance
  - needs to be visually striking and easily read

Posters
- posters can seem a little too propagandist, or patronizing, 'now wash your hands'
- siting is vital – you may want to choose restaurant and coffee areas as key sites, where people are more relaxed or test out the sightlines of people at various locations

- watch out for off-the-shelf posters: question if they talk the same language as your people
- posters can be quite a crude form of communication, only able to handle simple messages
  - they can be the internal communication equivalent of 'shouting', or there is a temptation to crowd them with far too much detail
- update all public display material regularly, otherwise it literally becomes wallpaper

Budget issues
- time spent updating notice-boards
- poster production

Timescales
- notice-boards can be updated almost immediately
- posters can be designed and printed in a few weeks

Activities
- set objectives
- updating notice-boards
- designing, printing and siting posters

Feedback
- 'open up' areas of notice-boards for free communication between people

Measurement
- awareness survey to see if key information has been spotted on posters and notice-boards
- monitor usage of notice-boards

How to find out more
- Take note of other people's notice-boards when you visit – develop a feeling for what makes a good or poor notice-board display

AWARD SCHEMES

Award schemes are long-standing ways of recognizing and rewarding people for appropriate behaviours and peak performance. They require intensive communication campaigns to support them, but the benefits are high in terms of both practical results and general motivation.

Strengths
- promoting involvement
- creating role models
- acting as a fast channel for good ideas

Opportunities
- combine with e-mail or multimedia to create on-line guidance for participants: for people who do not have access to a computer, create interactive kiosks in public areas
- involve potential entrants themselves in setting the standards and criteria for awards

Weaknesses
- can be demotivating for frequent, unrecognized submitters
- benefits hard to analyse

Pitfalls
- people feel their ideas have disappeared, or feel unrewarded for their effort
  - reply to all suggestions
  - send a holding letter if there is any delay in assessment
  - if an idea is not adopted, or a reward not given, write explaining why
- inconsistent reward
  - clear criteria and guidelines, or a central overseeing committee are needed to ensure that standard judgements are made and standardized rewards given
- *'whose idea was it anyway?'*
  - different people may come up with similar ideas, resulting in dispute
  - individuals might put forward ideas generated by their team
- *'surely it's just your job to do that?'*
  - it is difficult to set guidelines on where an award submission is merely someone doing their normal job, and where it is beyond the 'call of duty' and should be recognized

Budget issues	• setting up the scheme and administering it • communication campaign support
Timescales	• ongoing support for the system

Activities	• set objectives
	• research how best to run the scheme
	  – for example benchmark against leaders in the field
	  – for example find out what reward employees would value

Feedback	• survey employees to establish awareness of the scheme, reasons for participating or not participating, and the target behaviours and attitudes that are looked for
Measurement	• number of ideas generated • number of ideas implemented • cost savings or improvements made • proportion of target employees involved
How to find out more	The Industrial Society, Robert Hyde House, 48 Bryanston Square, London W1H 7LN 0171-262 2401

FOCUS GROUPS, SURVEYS AND RESEARCH

Successful internal communication rests on having a clear understanding of an audience and its needs. In the past, many organizations would have been content to rely on 'instinct'. Today, our more information-based society calls for conclusions based on research including full communication audits, regular attitude and opinions surveys, and focus groups to give a face-to-face dimension to research on specific issues.

Much depends on the statistical validity of the numbers and groups you sample, and ideally you need to cross-check different sources of data for validation. A mix of quantitative and qualitative research will give you 'meat on the bones' as you try to turn the findings of your research into practical communication. You should also take into account the need to compare data, either historically or with other organizations.

The important point to realize in this context is that doing research in itself communicates to your audience.

Strengths
- thorough and independent research will give credibility to your communication plan
- data can help convince management that the internal communication function is providing the strategic information it needs when determining change programmes
- research can generate attitude benchmarks against which future successes can be measured
- creates a forum for people to express opinion and suggestions
- makes people feel they have been consulted

Opportunities
- focus groups, as opposed to print surveys, bring people together, create links and enable people to swap ideas
- spot surveys give you an instant picture of how people are reacting to a particular issue
- surveys via e-mail give instant responses, and save having to input the data
- consider giving small incentives for people to do the research
  - for example stickers, pens and so on

- turn conclusions into a board presentation, gaining more visibility for yourself and demonstrating the strategic potential of communication activities

Weaknesses
- a thorough research project can be expensive and slow
- small sample sizes may be unrepresentative

Pitfalls
- not acting on issues raised
  - if the organization refuses to respond to concerns, it should at least explain why
- not feeding back the results
  - the natural assumption will be that the results were so bad you couldn't release them
  - ideally the full report on the results should be available on request
- unclear or ambiguous survey design
  - surveys always need to be tested on the target audience to make sure they generate the sort of output you need
- incomparable data
  - poor planning in determining what to measure limits the use of data, making it hard to compare with other data sources, or identify trends over time

Budget issues
- costs of research and feedback
- costs of communicating the results

Timescales
- a thorough opinion survey will take anything from two months and more to implement

Activities
- determine research objectives
- select research groups
- design research method
- carry out research
- analyse results
- feed back results to employees
- report results to senior managers
- take action on priority areas highlighted by research
- monitor improvement made in priority areas

Feedback
- keep an open door policy on research, with a clear contact point for unsolicited opinion and views on both content and method

Measurement
- historical data, for example changes in key attitudes
- benchmark against other organizations using similar research methodology

How to find out more
- contact organizations such as The Industrial Society for examples of research carried out by other companies

- check back whether any research has already been done within your organization

GRAPEVINE

Organizations tend to have a healthy respect for the grapevine. They recognize they can't destroy it, but they also fear that it will undermine the credibility of their own communication efforts – by painting a picture that internal audiences perceive as being the 'real' story.

In an ideal world, if as an organization you're being open and honest with people, the grapevine acts positively by *reinforcing* your messages, giving them added credibility in the language people use to talk.

Grapevines thrive where there's a communication vacuum – the perfect climate for sensational speculation, organizational paranoia, gossip, rumour-mongering and conspiracy theories.

The grapevine is there for social bonding and psychological needs as much as for an actual, deliberate need to share information. In fact, most organizations have multiple networks of grapevines, some of which will be entirely separate, restricted to specific social groups, professions or locations.

The grapevine needs to be included in any communication strategy as part of the media mix. You won't be able to control it, but you may be able to *influence* it, or at least predict and prepare for its impact. You can also act to circumvent it by creating even faster communication flows. In any event, you can't afford to ignore it.

Strengths
- highest credibility of any information source
- fast
- reaches everyone and in their day-to-day language
- acts as a 'safety valve'
- people select the information relevant to them
- personalizes messages, making them relevant to the listener
- highly reactive and interactive, a social medium
- can be used to give credibility to messages conveyed by formal communication methods

Opportunities
- open-door policy
  – you can work to become a focal point on the network
- establishing and demonstrating trust

        – building yourself into the network to monitor it
- encouraging formal grapevines
  - for example unedited free-form bulletin boards on the e-mail system, anonymous helplines, space on notice-boards
- providing fora for people to 'let off steam'
  - face-to-face meetings, making sure all media have places for anonymous feedback
- gauging opinion
  - attitude surveys (see focus groups etc., p. 136)
- internal recruitment
  - 'planting' forthcoming vacancies on the grapevine
- promoting informal behaviour change
  - dropping disciplinary hints, circumventing the need for more public and official disciplining

Weaknesses
- its weakness (or virtue, depending how you look at it) is simply that it *is* beyond management's control
- it is totally organic, and evolving continuously – by the time you've identified one grapevine route, another will have sprung up
- you have no control over who it reaches or when
- the grapevine may be stronger in particular parts of the organization, or have a differing bias
- there is a real danger of sensitive information leaking outside the organization

Pitfalls
- if you make the grapevine propagandist, you will look Machiavellian and untrustworthy
  - a new grapevine will simply bypass your own 'unreliable' one
- even if you do plant messages, there's no control over how they will be interpreted
  - there's a natural tendency to sensationalize and dramatize messages
- it can undermine the organization's formal structure and hierarchy and be used to destroy individuals

Budget issues
- time spent reviewing and feeding into grapevine

Timescales
- almost immediate

Activities
- set objectives
- sketching out informal communication flows
  - which routes do messages take?
  - are there people who are evidently key transmitters?
- testing timescales

- how long does it take for messages to reach different parts of the grapevine?
- promoting an open style of management
  - management by walking around etc. (see walking the talk, p. 18)
  - creating feedback mechanisms
- circumventing the grapevine
  - developing ever-faster methods of communication (see e-mail etc., p. 94, newsletters, p. 46, telephone and voice mail, p. 59, walking the talk, p. 18, moving light screens, p. 73)
- setting up crisis hotlines
  - special dedicated telephone lines with recorded messages or staffed to reassure callers

Feedback
- instant feedback via grapevine

Measurement
- how quickly messages are conveyed
- how effectively messages reach all target audiences
- how accurately messages are conveyed

How to find out more

Employee Communications and Consultation ACAS Publications, 1994

Effective Employee Communications by Michael Bland and Peter Jackson, Kogan Page, 1992

'Acknowledge and use your grapevine' by David Nicoll, *Management Decision*, **32**, (6), 25–30, 1994

IPD LIS Services, 25 Camp Road, Wimbledon, London SW19 4UX 0181-263 3355

Advisory Conciliation and Arbitration Service (ACAS), ACAS Public Enquiries, 83/117 Euston Road, London NW1 2RB 0171-396 5100

NETWORKING

Like the grapevine, networking is a valuable communication route, running up, down and across the organization, across sites and across functions. In contrast to the grapevine, however, networking is not primarily about passing on gossip or 'news', but about people seeking out individuals who have the skills, experience or information to help them.

Ideally, both partners will have something to gain from the relationship, looking for advice from each other, support and coaching, or simply someone to bounce ideas off.

The organization can encourage networking as a valuable development tool, an outlet for peers to consult each other, and an opportunity to share best practice across the organization.

Strengths
- people benefit from the skills and experience of others, regardless of their position in the hierarchy
  - meritocracy vs bureaucracy
- breaks down all barriers
  - functional, departmental, geographical, hierarchical, social
- marries well with the 'flattening' process most organizations are going through, and with the increased use of e-mail and other forms of computer networking

Opportunities
- promote networking in specific forms
  - for example mentoring
- encourage networking through training courses
- stress publicly that it is a valued skill
- extend networks out to customers and suppliers
- more active steps can be taken to facilitate networking where co-location of key people is impossible, for example providing dedicated teleconferencing or modem facilities

Weaknesses
- researching and building a reliable network takes a long time
- maintaining and using the network is time-consuming
- the network constantly changes shape and structure

- if you are bouncing ideas off someone lower than you in the hierarchy, it may be seen as a sign of weakness
- once someone on the network gives you advice, they may be surprised or offended if you don't take it
- the risk of ideas being stolen/opposed
- both parties have to see a clear gain in prospect
  - relies on 'enlightened self-interest', what's in it for me?

Pitfalls
- conflict can arise where someone powerful in the hierarchy is undermined by someone more skilled in the informal network

Budget issues
- networking tends to develop informally but you can invest in training and support to facilitate it

Timescales
- a full-scale network will take some time to develop, but relationships can start almost immediately

Activities
- set objectives, research and plan
- individuals build their own networks
- do what you can to ensure contact details are generally available

Feedback
- direct and immediate feedback between people on the network

Measurement
- no formal measurement but can be included as a general question in a survey of communication sources or looked at within an audit process

How to find out more
- set up informal conversations with line managers about the extent to which multidirectional contact does or does not take place
- explore whether such contact would add value, in their opinion
- look at existing communication and reference materials to assess the potential for facilitating networks

PUBLIC RELATIONS, NEWS MANAGEMENT AND MARKETING

Public relations, news management and marketing campaigns are key factors in the success of organizations in the public and private sector. It is essential that internal and external communication sends consistent and coordinated messages. Just as internal audiences are exposed to the organization's external communication, so the public may also gain access to internal communication.

In an ideal situation internal and external communication strategies are woven together, and there is close cooperation between the two areas of responsibility.

Organizations tend not to be proactive in news management and consequently the coverage tends to be a firefighting reaction to bad news. Attempts to get press coverage are still largely limited to press releases on new products or performance achievements. But *people* make a good story too, and in theory internal communication people are in the right position to identify them. News management also means that internal audiences should hear any news ahead of the media. All too often, the first internal audiences hear about job losses and site closures is on the television or radio news.

Strengths
- subliminal and cumulative effect of marketing messages
- external news is probably the most credible source of information
- reaches people through the media sources they choose

Opportunities
- set objectives
- involve everyone in public relation activities and stories, giving them credit for their work, for example invite them to suggest public relations ideas
- newsgatherers may want to add a human interest factor to stories, that is employees
- employees themselves do newsworthy things
  - expand personnel database to include likely candidates and their newsworthy activities

- give internal audiences on-line access to a database outlining the organization's position on key issues, and facts and figures about the organization's values, aims and performance
  - a cut down version could be used for induction purposes

Weaknesses
- public relations and marketing may be treated with some scepticism by some internal audiences
- the organization can trigger an initial interest from the news media but thereafter it's out of its control

Pitfalls
- *'do they mean us?'*
  - the image given by the news coverage may seem biased to an internal audience, creating resentment or cynicism
- *'they want to hear the real story'*
  - there may be unwelcome follow-up to any story that ignores the 'inside' view
  - the media is only too happy for whistleblowers to report the misdemeanours of their organizations

Budget issues
- time spent planning and coordinating internal and external communication

Timescales
- the demand for topicality determines a fast turnaround
  - the PR department may need quick access to 'newsworthy' employees to meet the needs of the media

Activities
- set objectives
- coordinating with, and supporting the PR department or suppliers to offer newsworthy material
- making sure that internal and external messages are consistent
- coordinating with marketing department to spread awareness of forthcoming marketing campaigns

Feedback
- evaluate as advertising

Measurement
- coverage of key messages in external media
- success of marketing campaign
- extent and quality of news coverage

How to find out more
Manage the Message: how to write communications that get the results you want by Bryan Thresher and Jim Biggin, Century Business, 1993
How to Understand and Manage Public Relations by D. White, Century Business, 1991

'Whose hand on the heartbeat?' by Jon White, *Human Resources*, Winter 1991/2

Institute of Public Relations, The Old Trading House, 15 Northburgh Street, London EC1V OPR 0171-253 5151

Chartered Institute of Marketing, Moor Hall, Cookham, Maidenhead, Berks SL6 9QH 01628 427500

ADVERTISING

Advertising – corporate, product and recruitment – strengthens the image internal audiences have of the organization. But this works both ways. Employees literally are ambassadors for their organizations – their behaviours have the potential to give the advertising credibility.

Strengths
- aligns external and internal views of organization
- high external profile/visibility
  - can add credibility and build pride
  - if positioned correctly, it is good news for employees, as it shows confidence and commitment on the part of the organization
- reaching internal audiences via the external media, usually when not at work
- reinforces internal messages
- helps to dramatize, personalize and demonstrate the organization's values

Opportunities
- involving employees in the advert's production
  - for example, real employees on screen or working to define the original concept
- employees and other relevant internal audiences should know in advance about advertising
  - this gives an additional feeling of being 'in' on something
  - prepares them to receive comments and questions from others

Weaknesses
- the advertising content may be treated with some scepticism
- it should not be used as a substitute for communicating direct

Pitfalls
- the reality gulf
  - internal audiences will become cynical if the picture painted in adverts is too idealized
- 'glitz'
  - there may be resentment at an obviously high advertising spend, especially at times of cost-cutting
- 'that's news to me'
  - people feel resentful and out of touch when the first they know about a new product, service or claim is when they're told about it in an advert

- *'what are we promising now?'*
  - very real worry that customers' expectations are being raised to unrealistic levels

Budget issues
- advertising is effectively free for internal communication purposes, though making people aware of forthcoming campaigns is an essential task

Timescales
- short timescales to coordinate advertising and internal communication campaigns

Activities
- set objectives
- make sure that internal and external messages are consistent

Feedback
- encourage internal audiences to comment on advertising

Measurement
- perception of company, organization, product or service by internal audiences before and after campaign

How to find out more

Advertising Excellence by C. Bovee, McGraw-Hill, 1994

Association of Graduate Recruiters, Sheraton House, Castle Park, Cambridge CB3 0AX 01223 356720
Institute of Practitioners in Advertising (IPA), 44 Belgrave Square, London SWX 8QS 0171-235 7020

Index